George W. Jones

George W. Jones

PRINTER LAUREATE

Lawrence Wallis

THE PLOUGH PRESS
MARK BATTY PUBLISHER

Published by The Plough Press
PO Box 8039
Nottingham NG5 2WN, UK
Web: www.ploughpress.com

First published in the United States of America
in 2004 by Mark Batty Publisher, LLC
6050 Boulevard East, Suite 2H
West New York, New Jersey 07093
Web: www.markbattypublisher.com

ISBN 0-902813-20-x (UK edition)
ISBN 0-902813-21-8 (special edition)
ISBN 0-9725636-7-9 (US edition)

Edited by Rachel Connolly
Designed by Andrew Shoolbred
Production by Geoff Barlow

(Frontispiece) George W. Jones at the age of 80

Set in Linotype Granjon and printed in Italy on
Gardapat 13 by Conti Tipocolor, Florence, Italy

British Library Cataloguing-in-Publication Data
A CIP Record is available from The British Library
Library of Congress Catalogue Number 2004111316

Contents

Preface 6

CHAPTER 1
Apprentice 9

CHAPTER 2
Journeyman 12

CHAPTER 3
Master Printer and Publisher 27

CHAPTER 4
Linotype and Miehle Machines 39

CHAPTER 5
Colour Printer 48

CHAPTER 6
Industrial Exile 57

CHAPTER 7
At the Sign of the Dolphin 61

CHAPTER 8
Printing Adviser 64

CHAPTER 9
Type Designer 69

CHAPTER 10
Book Collector 93

CHAPTER 11
Book Printer 99

CHAPTER 12
Jones and the Morison Circle 107

CHAPTER 13
Jones the Celebrity 111

CHAPTER 14
Retired Printer 120

Notes 122

Index 127

Preface

As an apprentice compositor in the 1940s and 1950s, I attended day-release and evening classes at the Department of Printing of the Camberwell School of Arts and Crafts in south-east London. It was at those classes that I first became aware of the name George W. Jones. He was mentioned *en passant* as the designer of the Linotype Granjon typeface, but his work was not lingered over, dissected and analysed to the same degree as that of his opposite number at the Monotype Corporation: Stanley Morison. Neither was he lauded as other type designers like Eric Gill, Jan Van Krimpen, Bruce Rogers or other notables of the twentieth century. Other aspects of his work were totally ignored. Reference books alluding to Jones are equally frustrating, the same limited information reiterated, sometimes with introduced errors.

Not until a couple of years ago was my interest in Jones rekindled when my friend Alan Hughes became the proprietor of Severnside Printers Ltd at Upton-upon-Severn in Worcestershire. One day, when making a desultory library reference on some other issue, I noticed, again *en passant*, that George Jones was born in the Severn Valley and in the very town where my friend was producing some quality printing. Alan was using offset-lithography (as most modern printers) and obtaining results that would not have shamed Jones had he employed the same process. Instead he printed by the now almost defunct letterpress process on Miehle machines from metal types, usually Linotype slugs.

This coincidence prompted me to produce a monograph on Jones: the first *book* on the subject. Alan, with customary enthusiasm, encouraged the idea, and the text that follows is the result. It has required a great deal of research and Alan has been helpful in respect of pursuing local Worcestershire connections with Jones, such as photographing his infant home in Court Street, Upton-upon-Severn, and in tracking down his apprenticeship indentures.

These were held by the Baylis family who owned the print works of Ebenezer Baylis & Son Ltd in Worcester where Jones received his trade training. Jones's links with the Worcestershire Regiment were also run to ground by Alan.

There are many other people who have given considerable assistance when delving into the elusive Jones. Quite by chance, I learned towards the end of 1992 that Professor Ian Rogerson, formerly Librarian at the Manchester Metropolitan University, had been collecting specimens of work printed by Jones for some years and was planning an exhibition early in 1993. We immediately began to exchange information and Ian allowed me to view the Jones collection in Manchester. His catalogue of the exhibition is a pioneering piece of work and ought to be tracked down by readers, especially those with keen bibliographical interests. The catalogue will be an essential guide for anybody contemplating a collection of work by Jones.

For access to correspondence between the American and British arms of the Linotype organisation concerning the development of the Baskerville (another Worcestershire-born printer) typeface, I am grateful to Martin Boothman, Managing Director of Linotype-Hell Ltd in Cheltenham, and to Steve Byers, formerly of the associated American company. I am also indebted to Roy Millington and T.G. Dakin for access to correspondence between Jones and John Northend of Sheffield. Permission to quote from this batch of letters was generously granted by T.G. Dakin, erstwhile Chairman and Managing Director of J.W. Northend Ltd in Sheffield.

At the St Bride Printing Library in London I was able to trawl the trade periodicals published during the working lifetime of Jones, an exercise that was greatly facilitated by the insights of James Mosley (the Librarian) and Nigel Roche of that excellent institution, which I have been visiting sporadically for the last forty years.

Others who have been of considerable help include the late and much-missed Walter Tracy, who, in certain respects, was the eventual successor to Jones in the Linotype company. His trenchant and expert opinions have been invaluable, both in conversation and through his excellent books *Letters of Credit* and *The Typographic Scene*. Such titles have gone some way to redress the imbalance between the welter of documentation for Monotype typography and the virtually negligible for Linotype typography. He also enabled me to purchase from him the catalogue of the second library of Jones at a price well below the true market value. It has been informative and invaluable when carrying out this work.

My thanks are due to Leon Symonds, former Head of the present incarnation of the Birmingham School of Printing, for allowing me to see the collection of Jones's work and memorabilia assembled years ago by Leonard Jay. His colleague Terry Coupland has also been of great assistance.

So many others have provided helpful advice: Alan Shelley, erstwhile of Linotype-Hell Ltd; the specialist booksellers Barry McKay (who first informed me about the work of Ian Rogerson), Tony Cox, Keith Hogg and Steven Tuohy; Colin Inman, the author of *The A. & C. Black Colour Books*; Annette and Tony Felgate, the latter a grandson of George W. Jones; Rupert Cannon; John Dreyfus for information on the International Typographic Council; Francine Corcione of the Jersey City Museum; Eric Gee, another former Head of the Birmingham School of Printing; Roger W.J. Slater, a local historian of Upton-upon-Severn; and the District of Malvern Records Office. As a septuagenarian with a failing memory, I apologise to those who may have assisted and been inadvertently overlooked.

Some explanation of the words 'Printer Laureate' in the title of this book may be appropriate. It was a description applied to Jones by *The Times* of London on the occasion of his seventieth birthday celebration. Such a distinction seemed apt, even if an understatement. His work was distinctive, exceptional and painstaking. He cared deeply about the printing industry, which I hope is reflected in the following pages. He contributed hugely to the elevation of printing standards in his day and full recognition has been withheld. I trust this book goes a little way to rectifying the unwarranted neglect.

Lawrence W. Wallis
Plymouth
Devon
2004

CHAPTER 1

Apprentice

Matthew Carter once remarked that the history of typography in the twentieth century has been largely written by the Monotype Corporation through the works of Stanley Morison, Beatrice Warde, John Dreyfus and others. That view is certainly sustainable from a British perspective. It helps to explain the relative neglect endured by some notable contributors to the industry outside that circle, such as George W. Jones, a London printer of considerable distinction and with many industrial credits to his name.

In his lifetime Jones was greatly admired and received widespread recognition for his work. Henry Lewis Bullen, the Curator of the Typographic Library and Museum of the American Type Founders Company, described him as 'the best all-round printer that Great Britain has ever produced. All that Bulmer, Baskerville, and the Whittinghams did he can do as perfectly.'[1] Bruce Rogers, foremost among American typographers, lauded him as that 'Master of Master Printers'.[2] J.R. Riddell, Principal of the St Bride Foundation Printing School, forerunner to the London College of Printing, referred to him in 1920 as 'probably the greatest living exponent of fine letterpress printing'.[3] Today his work has lapsed into near oblivion, being little known among the younger generations of printers and typographic designers.

George William Jones was born on 18 May 1860 at Upton-upon-

The house in Court Street, Upton-
upon-Severn, where Jones was born
and spent his childhood.

Severn in Worcestershire.[4] His father, George, was a blacksmith and
married Emma Clarke of Worcester on 3 June 1854 at St Martins
Church in the county town.[5] George W. Jones was the oldest child
and only son of the marriage and was baptised on 17 June 1860 at
Upton-upon-Severn.[6] Other children of the marriage were four
daughters: Alexandra Mary in 1863, Kate in 1864, Agnes Emily in
1867, and Jane in 1869.[7] Both the oldest and the youngest daughters
died in infancy. The family lived modestly at Court Street in the
centre of Upton-upon-Severn, a short walk from the river. George
W. Jones attended the National School in the town until just before
the age of eleven[8] when he was orphaned. His father died in 1868
and his mother in 1871.

Jones's attraction to printing as a potential career allegedly
occurred when seeing a schoolfellow 'in possession of a Great

Primer [roughly 18-point] letter' in type metal, which stimulated his imagination and led relentlessly to 'the [compositor's] case and printing press'.9 Leonard Jay, the erstwhile Head of the Birmingham School of Printing, wrote that the young aspiring printer 'walked six miles to buy his first dictionary' and showed an interest in letters at an early age, 'drawing those which appeared in the local newspaper'.10 Jones seems to have been generously endowed with that commendable Victorian ethos of self-improvement.

In 1872, at the age of twelve, Jones was recruited to the printery of Ebenezer Baylis & Son Ltd of Worcester as an odd-job boy, cleaning the workroom, providing manual power to drive a demy cylinder machine, rolling up ink at a handpress, running errands, and much else.11 His employer must have been sufficiently impressed by his industry and literacy to offer training in the trade on a more formal basis. On 24 March 1873 Jones signed an indenture as a printing apprentice with the firm for seven years' servitude to letterpress machine work and to handsetting of type. It pre-dated the more specialised training given in later years when an individual became either a compositor or a machine printer. His guardian, William Jones, an uncle and labourer from Northwick in the northern part of Worcester, witnessed the signing of the indenture.12

CHAPTER 2

Journeyman

SHEFFIELD

Owing to ill health (probably tuberculosis) suffered by Jones, Ebenezer Baylis agreed that the apprenticeship should be terminated prematurely in 1879 after six years, allowing the young journeyman to leave the trade for an open-air life in Derbyshire for recuperation. Thereafter Jones remained intensely proud of his Worcestershire heritage, steadfastly pointing out that William Caslon I and John Baskerville had similar roots. It is interesting to note, too, that Ebenezer Baylis & Son Ltd did not shrink from reminding the industry from time to time that George W. Jones began his illustrious career with the firm.[1]

In the autumn of the following year, Jones resumed in the printing industry at Sheffield and became a member of the Typographical Association (a trade union) on 23 October 1880.[2] He gained a variety of industrial experience in the north of England, starting at the jobbing department of the local newspaper, the *Sheffield Daily Telegraph*, and later as an overseer with Pawson & Brailsford Ltd, the 'substantial high class printers'.[3] In the last century the latter was equipped with letterpress, hand- and power presses and five lithographic machines driven by steam.[4] Jones left the company after a disagreement – a scenario that was to be repeated elsewhere. His last appointment in Sheffield was with Hartley & Son Ltd.

While in Sheffield, Jones forged some long-lasting friendships, notably with John William Northend (1855–1933), the founder of a family printing business in 1889. They corresponded regularly in the 1880s, particularly with reference to the *Printers' International Specimen Exchange*. Northend was strongly influenced by Jones when purchasing a Miehle machine in 1907 and when planning a new printing works in 1912.[5] Jones wrote affectionately of his friend in 1938: 'Dear John Northend, old, constant, and beloved friend. He was one of those printers in the eighties of the last century who thought no personal sacrifice too great or costly if so be they could in their work advance the craft to which they had consecrated their abilities'.[6] Later in life, Jones returned to the South Yorkshire city for special occasions, as when addressing the Sheffield Association of Master Printers in March 1925 on the subject of 'Craftsmanship and the Printer'.[7] It was during his stay in Sheffield that Jones married Eliza Sophia Ann Durham of New Whittingham, Derbyshire, in 1882. They probably met when Jones was seeking restored health in the county. His wife died at the age of fifty on 3 January 1912. She was buried at the Holy Trinity Church in Northwood, Middlesex.

LEICESTER

In 1883 Jones took up an appointment with Raithby & Lawrence of Leicester, at that time an unremarkable firm of commercial printers, which burgeoned into a much more distinguished enterprise. The association was to bring Jones into national and international prominence. His position with the firm has been variously described as 'works manager',[8] 'overseer',[9] and 'foreman',[10] the first probably being closest to actuality. With his appointment, the company was anxious to improve the style and quality of work produced.

Not unnaturally, Jones designed and worked in one of the favoured styles of the time, known somewhat affectedly as artistic printing. As Vivian Ridler has explained, the style represented 'the final attempt . . . by compositors to work out some kind of formula for jobbing design before the initiative was taken away from them'.[11] It was characterised by fancy and ugly alphabets in ill-assorted combinations accompanied by unrelated decorative borders and ornamentation, rules bent in all kinds of contortions, tint blocks and gaudy colour schemes. The style originated in America through the work of Oscar Harpel (Cincinnati 1870), but later more flamboyantly and emphatically with the efforts of William J. Kelly of the *American Model Printer* magazine, rivalled by John Earhart and Andreas Haight. The work was imported into Britain through the *Printers' International Specimen Exchange* of 1880 following a proposal by Thomas Hailing, a printer in Cheltenham and agent for, among other products, American periodicals. The scheme was promoted through the columns of *The Paper and Printing Trades Journal*[12] under the proprietorship of Andrew Tuer, a London publisher and printer preferring the Antique or Old Style of display founded upon the revival of various anachronisms and with Caslon revivalism as a mildly redeeming feature. Effectively the *Exchange* required offprints to be sent in by craftsmen at home and abroad, which were collectively bound up into volumes for circulation to the various contributors, the results providing a series of exemplars for emulation and improvement. Sixteen volumes of the *Exchange* appeared between 1880 and 1898 and constitute a rich seam of social and printing history.

Jones was an eager supporter and participant in the *Printers' International Specimen Exchange*. He was profoundly influenced by the work, especially by the 'brightness and originality of the American specimens'. In his own words they provided him with 'a new world to roam in'.[13] His work elicited frequent commendations for, as Ridler observed, the work of Jones in the style of artistic printing had 'an individuality lacking in most British jobbing printing'.[14] Early in 1889 a couple of plaudits were handed out. 'In display and ornamentation Mr. Jones has developed an entirely new style, using as a rule one or two faces of type only, relieved with a pretty initial, and very sparing use of ornament, and an occasional vignette introduced in a perfectly legitimate position.'[15] The same critic had earlier remarked, 'Bro. Jones . . . has developed . . . a wonderfully taking new style of design in which graceful type and ornamental combinations and dainty tinting rival each other in admirable effects'.[16]

It is easy for contemporary critics to be contemptuous of perceived absurdities, eccentricities and naiveties in artistic printing,

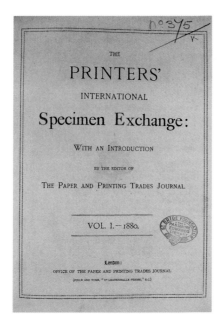

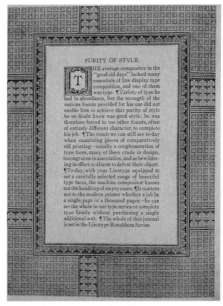

FIG. 2 (ABOVE)
Title page from the first volume of
the *Printers' International Specimen
Exchange*, 1880.

FIG. 3 (ABOVE RIGHT)
An apologia for artistic printing from
the *Linotype Record* of 1922. It was
probably written by Jones.

but the technical competence reached in hand composition was of a
very high order, as was the close register work on the platen press.
One must remember, too, that the compositors did not have routine
access to an extended series of sizes of a given type style or to families of variants of a given type design. Even the measurement of type
bodies was largely unregulated, which complicated composition. It
was not until 1886 that the American typefounders agreed to a standard measurement for the typographic point, and that was not
adopted by their British counterparts until twelve years later in
1898. One suspects that an anonymous apologia for artistic printing
may well have been written by Jones in a *Linotype Record* of 1922
pointing to deficiencies in composing resources. 'Variety of type he

had in abundance, but the strength of the various founts provided for his use did not enable him to achieve the purity of style he no doubt knew was good style; he was therefore forced to use other founts, often of entirely different character to complete the job.' The writer summarised artistic printing as 'usually a conglomeration of type faces, many of them crude in design, incongruous in association; and so bewildering in effect as almost to defeat their object'.[17]

Quite definitely, the typographic style eventually distilled by Jones towards the end of the nineteenth century (and by which he deserves to be remembered) owes little or nothing to artistic printing. Nonetheless, when at Raithby & Lawrence, Jones issued several booklets exhibiting various forms of job printing in the artistic style. Supplies of a book of specimens distributed at the end of 1887 were exhausted within a fortnight and were shortly 'changing hands at four times the published price'[18] of three shillings. His first couple of years in Leicester were spent reorganising the office, improving the methods of production, and extending the facilities of the firm and the scope of its work. He also helped to move the company in 1886 from Market Place to 16 Cank Street in Leicester, and the expansion continued with the acquisition of premises in Queen Street during 1888. Long after Jones departed for other work, Raithby & Lawrence became the focal point for avant garde typography, so much so that mature artistic printing became known as the Leicester Free Style.

At a testimonial in London on 15 January 1887 for Robert Hilton, celebrating his superintendence of the *Printers' International Specimen Exchange* since its inception, Jones proposed the idea of forming the British Typographia, an association of employing and working printers united in the aim of advancing vocational training throughout the industry.[19] The objectives were to form local branches, to establish libraries of reference and job specimens, to organise courses of technical instruction, to run seminars and group discussions, and to help settle trade disputes on appeal. Henry H. Bemrose was appointed President, with Jones on a Council of fifteen members, his employer J.C. Lawrence as Treasurer and Robert Hilton as Secretary. Undoubtedly the concept was forward-looking and progressive and turned out to be a success, with Jones leading the way in Edinburgh and London. It has been remarked that some of the British Typographia branches later developed into early schools of printing,[20] while others have noted that the organisation anticipated the Joint Industrial Council of 1919 which sought to promote industrial harmony and co-operation between employers and employed.

Some years later, in 1922, *The Caxton Magazine* reflected wistfully on the vision of the British Typographia and felt that a revival of its principles would be beneficial to contemporary industry. It enthused that the 'idea of the Typographia was magnificent, and it spread like a flame from Leicester all over the country'.[21] In reality, the rate of progress was a little more modest. The inaugural business meeting took place in Leicester on 1 August 1887 with Thomas Hailing serving as Chairman.[22] One outcome of the gathering was the preparation of a set of rules by Arthur Hurst of York.

At the first annual general meeting convened on 6 August 1888 at Cook's Temperance hotel in Leicester, the membership was reported to be 300, spread over thirty-eight towns from Preston to Plymouth and from Gravesend to Hereford and many locations beyond and between. Three branches had been formed in Bradford, Edinburgh (the work of Jones) and York.[23] At the next annual meeting, held in London at the Court Room of Stationers' Hall on 14 October 1889, the membership had increased to 1,000 and three new branches were in place at Birmingham, Glasgow and Manchester. Jones had been elevated from the Council to become a Vice-President.[24] For the rest of his life he actively encouraged printing education by serving on governing committees and by addressing groups of tradesmen and apprentices whenever business commitments permitted.

While Jones was in Leicester, Raithby & Lawrence launched *The British Printer*, a bi-monthly magazine which first appeared in January/February 1888. It was a publication that aspired to quality production, though its pages appear grey, weak and dull to modern eyes, being set in a descendant of Miller & Richard's Old Style of 1860 by Alexander Phemister.

Jones tended not to dissuade people from believing that he started *The British Printer*, but the evidence is contrary. In 1894 a legal dispute broke out between Raithby & Lawrence and Robert Hilton, the former seeking and obtaining an injunction against the

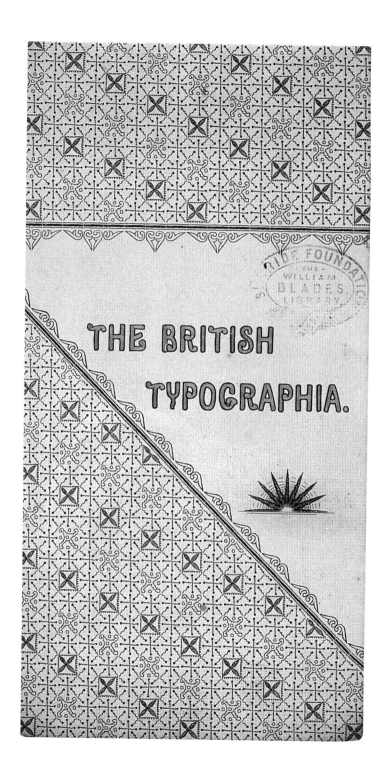

THE BRITISH TYPOGRAPHIA.

FIG. 4 (LEFT)
A folder produced in 1887 by Jones
to promote the British Typographia.

FIG. 5 (ABOVE)
Opening spread from the inaugural
number of *The British Printer*, January/
February 1888. It was the only issue
produced under the supervision of Jones.

latter for launching a magazine provisionally and variously named
The British Artist Printer and Lithographer, *The British Artist Printer*
and *The British Art Printer*, in competition with the established *The
British Printer*. Contained in the judgement are statements to the
effect that:

The British Printer seems to have been originally brought out by the defendant [Robert Hilton]. He carried it on for some years, and then the plain-
tiffs, Messrs. Raithby & Lawrence, joined their businesses together and *The
British Printer* was assigned to the firm. . . . When the company was formed

for the amalgamation of these businesses in 1890, an agreement of February 1890 was made by which it was expressly agreed that the defendant was to sell, and the Company was to purchase, the goodwill of the business carried on by him as publisher of *The British Printer*, and the copyright in it.[25]

Part of the settlement was that Robert Hilton could not engage in competitive activity for ten years. It is clear, therefore, that Robert Hilton had the original idea for *The British Printer*, fully supported philosophically and technically by Jones; Raithby & Lawrence provided the capital investment. Robert Hilton appears to have been a mercurial personality, teeming with ideas, if lacking in tenacity. He started several special-interest magazines soon after founding *The British Printer*, but they all failed. His powers of persuasion were immense, as Wilfred Lawrence was later to confirm. 'He had a golden tongue, and my father told me years afterwards that after all these new ventures had been started they were then left to him to manage until he [J.C. Lawrence] was completely overwhelmed.'[26]

From the outset, *The British Printer* was a keen promoter of artistic printing and the official mouthpiece for the British Typographia and for the *Printers' International Specimen Exchange*, taken over from Tuer. The experience of Robert Hilton in the last connection was crucial. He had edited *The Paper and Printing Trades Journal* for Field & Tuer Ltd over sixteen years.

Jones was responsible for producing the inaugural issue only of *The British Printer*, which proved to be a source of contention between him and his employers. It was caused by the lateness in delivery of the magazine, a problem that dogged Jones throughout his business life. Probably fastidiousness and a determination to produce perfect work caused the delays, though apparently not with *The British Printer*, where, according to Jones, the printed sheets languished awaiting binding because of the failure of Lawrence to attend to the matter. Robert Hilton joined the fray from his London office and everybody seems to have quarrelled, but the affair ended amicably over time as continuing cordial references to Jones in *The British Printer* testify.

Jones explained his reasons for leaving Leicester in a letter to John Northend:[27]

It was directly the result of No.1 *BP* in that Mr. Lawrence would see to the binding up and took three weeks to do it. During that time Hilton was unwell, and as I could not write him and say there were no more *BP*s ready I did not write for five or six days. I was rowing every day with Mr. Lawrence over the affair, but it was no use. The result was Mr. Hilton wrote a stiff letter to Mr. Lawrence, and then when he found he had gone too far, *put everything* on my shoulders. Not only did he do so, but in the most heartless way, not giving me a chance, or minimising the matter a bit. The result was neither Mr. L nor myself could get a line from him. The whole job was stopped, and I was so worried with the whole concern that I, having this job offered me, wh[ich] I at first refused, at last accepted. The result was that I wrote Hilton I was leaving R & L and he then, without writing or anything comes to Leicester, and as I was going home meets him in the street. We had a big row. He accused me of anything and everything, but having my assistant with me, I cleared myself entirely to his satisfaction, and he, seeing he had done me a great injustice, apologised for all his hasty and unkind language. The result is we are as friendly as ever, but after working R & L's business up as I did, pulling it out of the gutter, when they knew Grayson [Jones's successor] was secured, they, or at least *Mr. Lawrence*, the fellow I helped last Sept[ember] treated me something like a dog. So that I left without saying ta ta and have not yet written them.

For readers of *The British Printer*, the editor reported that Jones had been offered a better-paying job in Edinburgh.[28] Jones was a fiercely proud Victorian, a teetotaller,[29] a man of principle with a great capacity for friendship in spite of signs to the contrary. Right up to retirement in 1938 he remained in touch with fellow workers on *The British Printer,* such as Walter J. Beeby (compositor), Joey Darker (machine printer), and three apprentices: Billy Flint, Walter Clark and Harry Copeland. The magazine was printed on a Double Crown Wharfedale with a couple of Arab platens and a Golding Jobber for colour inserts.[30] Towards the end of his life Jones wrote:

I shall ever be glad that my steps were ordered, in the early twenties of my life, to Leicester, to take charge of the small printing office of Raithby & Lawrence in the old Market Place; and must be ever grateful for the trust and confidence both Mr. Raithby and Mr. Lawrence gave me; and for responding to my wishes and seconding my efforts in those days when a number of like-minded printers were endeavouring in their work, to the utmost of their opportunities, to express themselves in type and decorative material.[31]

Some measure of the esteem felt for Jones by his Leicester colleagues can be gauged from correspondence conducted many years later. Harry Copeland, writing on 14 September 1938 to Harry Whetton, then editor of *The British Printer*, explained:

I served the first half of my apprenticeship under that redoubtable crafts-man Geo. W. Jones and in those earlier days in Cank Street, he was no novice at colour work. Also he used to cut his own blocks and create his own colour combinations to enhance the beauty of those early productions. As I used to 'devil' for him when he was operating on the machine, washing up, mixing colour on ink table and all those details entailed in producing good print, I had a real good grounding in colour values over half a century ago.

From the same period, a letter from Joey Darker to Jones, dated 20 July 1938, testified to the professional leadership provided by GWJ: 'I think it is fifty-four years since we first met, when we was[sic.] in the middle of – I believe the last of Raithby & Lawrence's book almanacs, do you remember? and that old Irish tramp comp. who was setting the adverts. for same wasn't he just wild because you altered some of the pages he had set.'

EDINBURGH

On leaving Leicester in February 1888, Jones went to the Co-operative Printing Co.[32] at Bristo Place in Edinburgh. Despite public pronouncements of a higher salary, Jones received £4 a week,[33] the same sum he had averaged for the first three weeks of January 1888 at Raithby & Lawrence.[34] The company in Edinburgh employed eighty people and operated seven cylinder and two platen presses.[35] It appears that earlier the proprietor had fallen out with the princi-pals of the Co-operative Society, causing them to establish a large printing house in neighbouring Glasgow to service their publishing requirements and leaving the press in Edinburgh short of work.[36] Accordingly, Jones was approached as a person who might be able to fill the shortfall of business, and the name of the enterprise changed to the Darien Press. He was put in charge of a special department for 'Artistic Work',[37] and produced a number of speci-mens of work in this genre while in Edinburgh. Critical accolades followed, as in *The British Printer* of 1888:

The invigorating air of the north seems to have had a refreshing effect on Mr. Geo. W. Jones, who still finds time amidst his increased duties as overseer of the Co-operative Printing Company Limited, Edinburgh, to send us occasional collections of specimens – we had almost said 'of his handiwork', but of this he is now happily relieved, his duties as regards these consisting of sketching designs for others to follow, and superintending their productions. The finished execution of all the specimens before us show that he is well supported by his staff, and by the Assistant Foreman, Mr. A. Wilson, and Mr. Lamont, Overseer of the Machine Department. Mr. Jones has developed a new style of display in which plain rules and simple line ornaments are gracefully combined, invariably with chaste effect.[38]

The same critic remarked a couple of months later:

Mr. Geo. W. Jones sends us from his northern retreat . . . half-a-dozen specimens bearing the genuine hallmark of his cultivated taste and skilful accurate finish. We have marked a couple of them for reproduction as soon as occasion offers. . . . Mr. Jones has for sale on very moderate terms a few collections of his best specimens done during the past two years (mounted and bound in quarto albums, each containing about two hundred specimens, mostly in colours), any one of which would be a perfect treasure trove to an aspiring printer desirous of improving his productions.[39]

Harold Hood, writing some years later in *The British Printer* of 1920, reflected on an advice card printed in 1888/89 by Jones at, and for, the Darien Press. He observed that his style, even then, was 'highly graceful' and went on to expand the theme:

He did not scorn ornament but used it with considerable restraint, despite the specimens to the contrary of its nearly always German originators.

If Keats' 'A thing of beauty is a joy for ever' were strictly true, then you could only prove 'beauty' by ascertaining at the end of 'for ever' whether it were still then a joy. This [early advice card] must now be regarded as not of these times, and yet I confess to admiration of it for some reasons, because in it there are attributes of gracefulness and of a certain suitability.

Yet fashion goes for much, and I am quite certain that Mr. G.W. Jones (may his shadow never grow less) would not issue such an advice card of his own these thirty-two years later, as the one I am discussing. It would almost certainly be entirely devoid of ornaments, and the lettering would be quite clear – which in this one certainly is not. Perhaps I should not say entirely devoid of ornaments, but such as there might be would probably be specially designed for the job.

There can be no real art where special and complete and *exclusive* decoration does not govern the whole scheme; and since Mr. Jones's wonderful examples of the '80s and '90s, his evolution has taken the course of throwing over 'stock' ornament as far as possible, with a tendency towards greater and greater restraint with corresponding increasing purity and simplicity of style.

I have long regarded G.W. Jones as the greatest typographic artist in this country. It is a privilege to acknowledge his influence upon me. I worked under him twenty-eight years since, and no technical experience affected my life more than the close influence of that strong character then.[40]

In addition to daily commercial duties in Edinburgh, Jones formed a branch of the British Typographia and taught evening classes for typography in conjunction with the University Preparatory Institute. The instruction was undertaken in the lecture hall of Minto House and nearly 100 students attended.[41] Concurrently, a similar class in typography had been projected by the Heriot Watt College under the direction of James Wilkie.

There appears to have been a competitive element in establishing the two classes – at least from the perspective of Jones. He wrote privately on the matter towards the end of his life:[42]

The management of the Heriot Watt College, then one of the finest technical institutions in the world, decided to establish a class for printers in the early autumn of the year 1888.

A Mr. Murdo McLeod, a clever coach in certain University subjects, and who rented a few very small rooms, told a printer friend he would like to copy the Heriot Watt idea, and asked him if he could recommend an instructor. He advised him to 'try and get that young English fellow who had recently gone to the Darien Press' as it was then named, as he seemed to be a very progressive printer. The result was that I consented to endeavour to establish a class, although I had only been in Edinburgh two or three months. I arranged to have my first meeting the evening before the Heriot Watt instructor – a man well-known in Edinburgh – held his. The result was that the largest room, which could only hold sixteen or eighteen people, was filled when I arrived, as were the passages and other rooms. Only six or eight signed on as members – Scottish-like waiting until they had heard Mr. Wilkie, the Heriot Watt instructor, the next evening.

Getting hot on the job I wired my friend Hilton in London, and with my own collection, held an exhibition on the Saturday of the same week in a room specially hired for the purpose. We got a dear old Edinburgh working printer to open the Exhibition, which was wonderfully successful – so much so that after some talkee-talkee by myself some seventy or eighty fine fellows joined the class. They consisted of the flower of Edinburgh printerdom, men occupying fine positions, as well as several keen but small master printers, who brought some of their staff with them. The principal students took the bit in their teeth and demanded the best lecture room they could get in Edinburgh for our meetings. We ultimately met in the fine operating theatre of Minto House, and numbered ninety-seven students. They forced the hand of McLeod, and told him that if he did not accede to their wishes, they would make it their class. They said to me 'Mr. Jones, keep out of the arrangements for a lecture room. We will see to this. You see, you are only an Englishman, and our friend Murdo is "Hieland", and it will take us southern Scots all our time to get what we intend to procure for you; that is, a room worthy of this big class.'

Oh, but they were great, right from the first night. There never has been, and never will be, such a class again!

The exhibition of printed specimens referred to by Jones was held on Saturday 29 September 1888. It had an international dimension with work from Austria, Germany, America, Australia, China and elsewhere. Hilton had clearly responded enthusiastically to Jones's request for examples of work, the source being the *Printers' International Specimen Exchange*. On Wednesday 3 October 1888, Jones conducted his first typography class in Edinburgh. It was followed on Tuesday 9 October 1888 by the inaugural lecture of Wilkie at the Heriot Watt College, attended by some sixty students.[43]

In January 1889, Jones organised another exhibition of fine printing at the Literary Institute in Edinburgh which ran for three days. Again the work shown was of an international character, the specimens from America and Germany being much admired. Contributory local specimens were to be sent to his home at 7 Roseneath Terrace in Edinburgh, or to the offices of *The British Printer* or the residences of two committee members.[44] Formal opening of the exhibition was performed by Archibald Constable of the firm T. & A. Constable. Without doubt, the exhibition was an unqualified success and exerted a considerable influence on those who attended.

On Saturday 8 June 1889, the members of the Minto House classes in typography met socially to mark the end of the first academic session and to say farewell to Jones. Seemingly the classes had secured outstanding support with the enrolment of ninety-seven students; thirty-one meetings had been convened throughout the session with an average attendance of seventy, and forty-six students sat the examinations of the City & Guilds of London Institute.[45] In front of the gathered students and distinguished guests, including Robert Hilton, Jones was presented with a clock bearing the inscription: 'Presented to Geo. W. Jones by the members of his typography class, as a mark of their admiration of his high character and professional abilities'. Among the appreciative remarks made by the Chairman for the occasion, Alex Weir testified to the beneficial influence of Jones in having 'been the means of almost revolutionising job printing in Edinburgh'.

Among his students in Edinburgh was William Maxwell, later Managing Director of the respected book house of R. & R. Clark Ltd, the printers for the works of George Bernard Shaw, an author with firm typographic predilections.[46]

Jones returned for a visit to Scotland a few months later. On Wednesday 16 October 1889, he distributed medals and prizes to his old students at Minto House[47] and went on to deliver an introductory lecture on Saturday 19 October 1889 to the freshly-formed printing classes in Selkirk. W.B. Grieve, the overseer of the *Southern Reporter* office in Selkirk, was the instructor and a former student of Jones.[48] The proprietors of the Borders newspaper, George Lewis & Son Ltd, asserted in 1891 that the 'real beginning of our career as fine printers dates from the time of the Edinburgh Exhibition of fine printing, the result of the enthusiasm of the Minto House (Geo. W. Jones) Class of Typography'.[49]

CHAPTER 3

Master Printer and Publisher

By the middle of 1889, Jones had removed from Edinburgh to London for reasons unknown. He next turned up as Works Manager for the Grapho Press at Creechurch Buildings, Leadenhall Street, in the City of London. That Jones was a prize scalp for the company can be seen in press advertising, with his name emphatically displayed and trumpeted.[1] Almost immediately *The British Printer* was noticing specimens from the firm and remarked that 'Mr. Jones's inventive faculty is as progressive as ever'.[2]

Writing on Grapho Press notepaper to John Northend on 26 July 1889, Jones indicated the readiness of some trade cards for the Sheffield printer, probably in connection with the founding of a new family business. He explained that two or three advance cards had been enclosed and that the bulk supply had been 'done but not yet dry'. His spirits appear to have been high. He indicated that the Grapho Press was undergoing expansion with the imminent installation of a 'four-horse gas engine and a Double Demy Wharfedale . . . also electric light'. He added, 'I am anticipating we shall be fairly well off for work. Two travellers, one out for us entirely, another on commission. The prospect is fair, though expenses will be very heavy for a first year off. Still, I am full of bright hopes and I feel better than I have done for twelve months.'[3] He was living at 48 Chetwynd Road, Highgate, London, during this period.[4]

Fine Printing for the Trade.

THE GRAPHO PRESS is stocked with the newest and most artistic faces of English, American, and German Type and Borders. The Machinery is specially designed for the production of the Finest Art Printing, and Mr. GEO. W. JONES, late of the Darien Press, Edinburgh, has undertaken the management of the Works. THE GRAPHO CO., LIMITED, are confident that in inviting the Trade to favour them with orders for any specially fine work, for the production of which ordinary plant and machinery may not be suited, the result will be eminently satisfactory.

⁘ Creechurch Buildings, Leadenhall Street, LONDON, E.C. ⁘

FIG. 6
On moving to London in 1889,
Jones was recruited as Works
Manager of the Grapho Press.
Advertising in the trade press
trumpeted the appointment.

One significant encounter occurred at the Grapho Press with Edward Shanks, the typefounder. He had sought out Jones to print some jobs. Jones recalled, 'I well remember his making himself known to me at a little printing office off Leadenhall Street on my coming to London in the summer of the year 1889; the commencement of a lovely and inspiring friendship . . . His practical training as a printer, for his wise Scottish father insisted on his apprenticeship to the business, stood him in good stead during his career as a practical typefounder.'[5]

After a few months, Jones resigned from the Grapho Press to establish a business on his own account at 20–22 St Bride Street in the environs of Fleet Street, trading under the title of Geo. W. Jones, Fine Printer to the Trade.[6] One can only speculate on the reasons for Jones severing contacts with the Grapho Press after such a short time. He may have been galvanised by the news that John Northend was starting up in business independently, as the two had disclosed a friendly rivalry in correspondence. It seems difficult to believe that Jones had become disaffected with the Grapho Press when seen in the context of the euphoric letter to Northend of July 1889, yet that appears to have been the case, as Jones recollected in February 1927:

Finding my position uncongenial, I soon afterwards terminated my agreement, left the eastern part of the city, and, deciding to start business on my own account in what was then to me a great wilderness of bricks and mortar, I made my way to 31 Red Lion Square, the scene of the life-work of my friend [Edward Shanks]. I remember as if it was yesterday his expression of surprise at my visit, for he usually came to see me. I told him that I had parted from my friends in the city, and that, without even knowing the name of the street until after I had agreed to rent part of a room on the second floor of a large building, I had decided to commence in St. Bride Street. All that I had known or really cared previously was that the street radiated from Ludgate Circus. I shall never forget his ready and personal encouragement, for, before anything further was said, he remarked, 'Of course, you know it was to you I came, and not to the friends with whom you were associated!'[7]

The British Printer almost contained a note of relief when reporting that Jones had decided to go it alone, perhaps because he had been hinting strongly to Robert Hilton of the possibility for some considerable time. 'Our readers will notice from an announcement on another page that Mr. Geo. W. Jones has at last taken the final plunge and commenced business on his own account . . . He has laid down modern machinery, the latest artistic types and borders, and labour-saving appliances, and is prepared to undertake fine printing for the trade. Original designs and superior work guaranteed with prompt attention.'[8]

Not unnaturally, the enterprise had modest beginnings, occupying 'part of a room' with 'one man and one machine and a boy', as Jones later recalled.[9] Following the elapse of a few months, he advertised for an apprentice, preferably 'one with a taste for drawing'.[10] The trade press was quickly remarking on the progress of the company. 'Mr. Geo. W. Jones, who only a few months ago commenced business . . . appears to have "struck ile" at once. Himself and staff have had all and more than they could do from the start, and he has within the last month extended his premises and added two new machines and a quantity of new material to his office, which is a model of neat arrangement and replete with modern labour-saving appliances.'[11]

In October 1889, the International Exhibition of Fine Printing was held at Stationers' Hall in London. It had a grand opening ceremony attended by the Lord Mayor and Lady Mayoress. Jones was a member of the party supporting the Chairman and had the distinction of past association with three of the five companies receiving awards in the First Class, namely the Darien Press of Edinburgh, the Grapho Press of London, and Raithby & Lawrence of Leicester.[12] Jones never shunned publicity. On the contrary, he tended to court it and on this occasion had clearly exhorted erstwhile principals to enter some of his work for judgement.

Jones's interest in technical education remained unabated on reaching London, where a Metropolitan branch of the British Typographia was formed. He taught typography classes twice a week at separate City locations attended by some 177 students.[13] His opening lecture occurred on Thursday 3 November 1889 at the Bishopsgate Ward Schools in Primrose Street and was presided over by a representative of the London County Council. On the following Tuesday he conducted his first class at the Board School, Greystoke Place, Fetter Lane, under the Presidency of Henry Bemrose. Thereafter the two classes were held weekly which must have been something of a strain for Jones with the added responsibility of establishing a new business.[14]

On Saturday 4 January 1890, the second session of classes was launched with a social evening at the Champion Hotel, Aldersgate Street, in the City. More than 100 students attended. Jones presided over the proceedings and the usual extravagant social exchanges of the time took place throughout the supper,[15] with everybody receiving a pat on the back. The following June, the students expressed gratitude for the work of Jones with the presentation of a writing cabinet inscribed with the words: 'Geo. W. Jones, a mark of appreciation from Students of City Metropolitan Classes, London, June 9th 1890'.[16]

Jones's connection with the venture lasted only for a short time afterwards because of the need to consolidate and expand a fledgling business. Nonetheless, he continued to lecture widely on an occasional basis throughout the country for years. One of the more distinguished students in the London classes of Jones was W.H. Slater,[17] who went on to instruct at the Borough Polytechnic and wrote a manual called *What a Compositor Should Know,* published in 1930.

The year 1891 was an important one for Jones. His business was moved from 20–22 St Bride Street to more spacious premises at number 35 (see colour illustration 1). Furthermore, he struck up an association with *The Printing World*, a monthly trade magazine started in January 1891 and commanding an annual subscription of five shillings (equivalent to 25 pence). It was originally produced by Unwin Brothers, though Jones frequently printed colour inserts and supplements from an early date. In the April 1891 issue, a displayed announcement proclaimed that Jones would print four pages of the magazine, starting with the May issue.[18] Over time the relationship became closer, as evidenced by an editorial in the January 1892 issue stating that George W. Jones would in future print the whole periodical. It was added prophetically that the next issue may 'be a little late'.[19] Not only was the February appearance delayed, but the March deadline was also missed.

John Bassett (1863–1892), publisher and editor of *The Printing World*, was stirred by frustration to comment on the late delivery in the columns of March 1892:

Friend Jones is a hard man to tackle, and he could talk a mother-in-law into his way of thinking. This is how I am treated when I visit 35 St. Bride Street: I say, 'Well, Friend Jones, you are late again *as usual*, what is the meaning of it?' and he looks up as innocent as if he didn't know what you were talking about, and remarks, 'Ah, Friend Bassett, I am not going to spoil the appearance of the book even if I am three or four days late, and I mean to keep the sheets until they are dry.'[20]

Readers' complaints about tardiness were again acknowledged in May and some years later in September 1895. Jones's quest for perfection was in conflict with promptness of delivery on many occasions. He never overcame the problem, even on undeniably time-critical work. His calendar for 1922, incorporating a process colour illustration, was late and accompanied by a sanguine note: 'With compliments. Trusting that the opinion of our friends will be "Better late than never".'[21]

Despite delays in the publishing schedule, the readership of *The Printing World* appreciated the enhanced quality brought about by Jones's production. Several plaudits were contained in the March 1892 issue. John Lewis of Selkirk extended: 'Warmest congratulations on

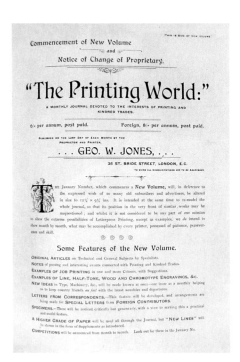

the immense improvement you have made in the typography of *The PW*. Its handsome dress of Ronaldson OS., its beautifully displayed advertisement pages, the original blocks and vignettes at the head of chapters, give the journal a fresh and thoroughly artistic appearance. It reminds one of some of the best American trade papers, only the display pages are more original and much more effective.' James Silsbury of Shanklin on the Isle of Wight offered, 'Hearty congratulations on your first number of *The PW*. Must admit I rather expected to see a little of the signs of rush in the machining of the first issue – but my copy is perfect!' Somewhat ingenuously and charmingly, J.T. Steele of the paper merchants Spicer Brothers Limited, commented, 'My brother, who is a practical printer, says your paper is the best going. It is *the master* production.'[22]

In December 1892 John Bassett died and Jones contracted to buy *The Printing World*, which took effect with the first issue of 1893 (see colour illustration 2). With proprietorial publishing and printing

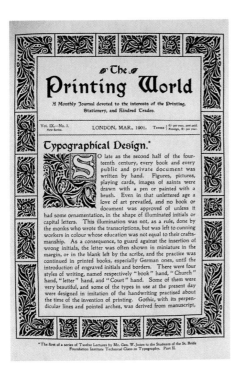

FIG. 8
Jones experimented with various typographic design styles in the pages of *The Printing World*, before settling on a model that owed much to the work of William Morris at the Kelmscott Press. This page from the March 1901 issue demonstrates the point.

interests at the age of thirty-three, Jones's career flowered. He advertised trade services of 'Superior Printing'[23] and 'Fine Printing'[24] in the pages of *The Printing World*, and by 1898 added a speciality for 'fine half-tone and illustrated work'.[25] Ian Rogerson has correctly stated that as 'a vehicle for advertising his own skills and as a means of keeping up-to-date with new developments, the journal stood him in good stead'.[26] His printing company undertook a wide range of jobbing work, as well as periodical and book printing. This broad approach contrasted with other distinguished presses in the history of the trade which have tended to specialise in a single and narrow area of print production, notably books. Success attended the policy with a move in 1897 to larger premises at St Bride House, Dean Street, Fetter Lane, still in the locality of Fleet Street.

One senses in the pages of *The Printing World* that Jones was experimenting typographically and striving to settle on a 'personal' style. It is possible to detect diverse influences in his work of this period, such as Artistic Printing, Art Nouveau, and the Arts and Crafts Movement. His quaint printer's marks of this period reveal some of these visual forces and contrast sharply with the neater and cleaner Aldinesque devices of later work. With the early issues of *The Printing World* in 1901, I surmise that the typographic style nowadays associated with George Jones began to crystallise, exemplified by: a predilection for ornate initial letters; the use of decorative page borders, headpieces and tailpieces; a preference for Venetian typefaces; and an overall ambience of allusive and derivative typography. He was reported in 1897 as renouncing artistic printing: 'Mr. Jones stated that they were coming to a style that was simpler and purer than that which was in vogue eight or nine years ago. He contended that fine printing paid, but if by fine printing they meant many colours and highly ornamental, he thought there was nothing so undesirable.'[27]

My belief is that Jones was profoundly influenced by the work of William Morris at the Kelmscott Press: the two men did meet as Jones mentioned in numerous public lectures. In 1924, *The Caxton Magazine* attended a meeting in London addressed by H.L. Bullen and chaired by Jones. The latter was reported as follows:

He remembered John Bassett came to him and said, 'Jones, look at that.' It was a copy of one of the first books by William Morris. He saw then that he knew nothing whatever about printing. He never had the opportunities that William Morris possessed. . . . [who] was wealthy and a genius. He went down to see him one day. Morris said, 'I suppose you are not going to keep me long?' But later he was a bit more affable, and by and by they were going through his books. He told Morris that he wanted to buy some of his books. For a Socialist he never saw a man with a bigger eye to the main chance. When he was going he asked William Morris if he knew why he had bought his books. Morris supposed it to be for the same reason as other people did. He replied that was not so. During all his leisure and his working hours Morris had shown in his books all he had been able to extract with his genius and feeling, and had put it all into these two or three books, and that was why he was buying them. He could get in that concentrated form all Morris had been able to find out about printing.[28]

Some months later, the same journal reported that 'Jones recalls with pride his meeting with William Morris, and dates his regeneration as a printer from that happy occasion. From Morris he learnt the lesson of simplicity, and translated it into a form applicable to commercial needs.'[29] Simplicity is not the first word that comes to mind when thinking of Kelmscott productions, but compared to artistic printing the force of Jones's argument becomes clearer.

Speaking to a gathering of printers in Sheffield during 1925, Jones paid full tribute to the work of William Morris at the Kelmscott Press.

To William Morris . . . must be given much of the credit for the great advance which set in and has been growing since the year 1891 towards purer, simpler, and more beautiful typography. Many of us, even those who had for years been more or less single-mindedly giving time and strength to the advancement of our calling, will never forget the day when the first of Morris's books was placed in our hands. For myself I realised how little I knew, how great a fool I was, and how much I had to learn even after so many years of serious work. I sought an introduction to the master craftsman; to the man who, by patient labour in the mastering of detail, by his type design, his interview with papermakers, his experiments with paper and vellum, his careful inquiries into the manufacture of ink, his watchful collaboration with Mr. Emery Walker, and with Mr. Edward Prince who cut his punches, and by his finished work, became in its highest sense the master printer craftsman. I saw him at his house in Hammersmith and he told me that he decided to print because of his love of beautiful typography, and because the form of type which he could approve would not carry sufficient ink to satisfy his idea of a perfect book face. He showed me many of the treasures of his library – the second library he formed. I remember so well the reverent care with which he handled each volume and pointed out the beauties of each and the suitableness of the types, specially of the fifteenth-century German printers for the printing of fine books, and described the features of bookmaking which impressed him most strongly.[30]

Jones became a keen collector of antiquarian books, which he used as models for his own work. My suspicion is that the habit of book collecting was inspired by the encounter with Morris, as hinted in a lecture given to the Faculty Club of the University of California during 1930.

He [Morris] told me that he was first led to design and make his own types because he could not procure them from the recognised typefounders of sufficient strength of face, or possessing the character that appealed to him most strongly. He seemed to take great pleasure in showing me the books which had helped him in deciding upon his type forms, as well as those which had specially influenced him in the matter of margins, decoration and illustration. He had one little mannerism: he would, on opening a book, take his red pocket handkerchief and gently flick the back of the opening, so as to remove any dust which might have accumulated. After he had given me the information I had specially sought, and after I had purchased some of his works, he inquired why I had bought them.

I explained that I had never had the opportunity of studying books such as he showed me, and that I never hoped to be able to afford to buy even one or two of them. That even if I could, I could not hope to see in them all that he had been able to see and extract from them by his study and knowledge, and that it seemed to me in his printed books, each one specially designed, with its individual treatment, in the manner of size, margins, choice of letter, decoration, and illustration, he had focused all his knowledge of the art and science of the book ...

I told him that to a busy man the possession of those books was in some ways more valuable to me even than his library. He seemed pleased at my frankness, and also that I should be taking that means of study in order that I might apply as far as possible the lessons I might derive from it to my everyday work.[31]

Without question, *The Printing World* was the best of the British trade journals of the time in terms of quality of design and production, and editorially was livelier and more venturesome than its competitors in the guise of *The Caxton Magazine*, *The Printers' Register*, the *British Colonial Printer and Stationer*, and even *The British Printer*, which aspired to quality but could not match the technique of Jones. *The Printing World* was not out of place among the superior contemporary American periodicals such as the *American Model Printer* and *The Printing Art*. It used the best available typefaces of the period that had some character and verve, such as Ronaldson Old Style, Cheltenham Old Style, Caslon Old Face, Clearface, and the better versions of Old Style and Modern. One must bear in mind that the great typographical revival programmes had still to be enacted by Stanley Morison at the Monotype Corporation Ltd and by Jones himself at Linotype & Machinery Ltd. Special designs were commissioned for 'headpieces, initials, panels, and various other ornaments suitable for the embellishment of letterpress work', as announced in the December 1894 issue which contained some new work by J. Hutchison. The pages of *The Printing World* were clear, legible, and enticed the reader. Its style was restrained and uncluttered but interesting. The subject matter was relevant and challenging, notably the articles dealing with design and layout. Jones gave up the magazine some time in 1908 for reasons that will become clear later, and the title limped on for another three years with progressive blandness until September 1911. *The Printing World* was a watershed in the career of Jones and enhanced his reputation.

Some notion of Jones as an employer can be deduced from the pages of *The Printing World*. He advertised for an apprentice fairly regularly in the 1890s, but insisted that a premium had to be paid by the family of the boy when that trade practice was declining.[32] He clearly felt that the training given at Geo. W. Jones Ltd was worth the investment. His attitude as an employer seems to have been resolute, fair, and somewhat enlightened for the time. Activities of *The Printing World* cricket club featured regularly in the pages of the journal, with Jones prominent at social events and matches.

In November 1897, a smoking concert was held for members at the Falcon Hotel in Gough Square, with Jones in attendance as Honorary President and with Joey Darker chairing the proceedings. In April 1898, a staff dinner was given by the firm at Stone's Hotel off Ludgate Hill and some sixty people attended, with Jones presiding after a 'severe illness'.[33] The event was organised to celebrate the earlier move by the company to 'spacious new premises' in 1897. Hampton Court was the destination for the wayzgoose of *The Printing World* in July 1901, which culminated with a dinner at the Cardinal Wolsey Hotel. Jones thanked the staff of St Bride House 'in all departments, not only for the excellence [of their work], but for the splendid loyalty of their service. The one quality in a worker that he valued above all others was loyalty, for however good a printer a man might be, he was of no permanent value if he could not be depended on at a pinch.'[34] Jones certainly engendered enthusiasm for the trade and inspired loyalty in his employees, as enduring professional relationships testify throughout his life.

Jones's employees were encouraged to participate as fully as possible in the trade and to develop their skills. They can be found contributing articles to the trade press and winning prizes in competitions. An example of the latter occurred in 1907 when 'Mr. A.E. Henley (with Messrs. Geo. W. Jones Ltd, Watford) has been declared the winner of the first place, with a prize of £5, in the London Society of Compositors' trade card competition, with a design which the judge (Mr. H. Whetton, editor of *The British Printer*) describes as "neat, useful, effective, and workmanlike". The competition was open to all members of the LSC., and seventy-three designs were submitted.'[35]

Jones was a generous and paternalistic employer. Yet he was not a soft touch for the workers, as Angus Wiltshire, a compositor, discovered in 1899 when suing Jones for two weeks' wages in lieu of notice of dismissal. His action was supported by the London Society of Compositors. Jones won the judgement and wrote a trenchant editorial on the matter in *The Printing World* of May 1899. He was particularly censorious of the role of the trade union in sustaining the complainant. He wrote:

> . . . the committee of the London Society of Compositors, or the executive body of any other trade union whatsoever, is so weak-kneed and invertebrate as to be incapable of denying moral and financial support to frivolous, rash, or impudent litigants, if it plays to the gallery or panders to the mob by lightly allowing the union's funds to be squandered by any combative or cantankerous member who chooses to trump up a flimsy and vexatious action against an unoffending employer – then farewell to the influence and power of that union, whether it be a union of compositors or of cattle-drovers. Trade unions ought not, for their own sakes, to busy themselves in adding to the burdens of trade by rendering more difficult and harassing the already too severely strained relations between employer and employed.[36]

CHAPTER 4

Linotype and Miehle Machines

Jones drew abiding sustenance from the visual style of Morris, but the two men had vastly differing attitudes to technology. As a businessman, Jones seized the opportunities provided by new methods of production; he was in the vanguard of change. His reputation is founded, among other things, on the virtuoso use of the Linotype and Miehle machines.

LINOTYPE

The earliest reference I have found[1] to Jones employing a Linotype machine is contained in the imprint of the book *Progress in Printing and the Graphic Arts during the Victorian Era* by John Southward, dated 1897. It reads: 'The whole of the Roman Type in this Book has been set up by the Linotype Composing Machine, and machined direct from the Linotype Bars by Geo. W. Jones, Saint Bride House, Dean Street, Fetter Lane, London E.C.' It was only seven years earlier in 1890 that the first Linotype machine came into commercial operation in the United Kingdom at the *Leeds Mercury*. Jones could scarcely have been quicker off the mark, since the invention did not really settle down until approximately 1892 or a little later.[2] Additionally, the Linotype machine made faster inroads into newspapers

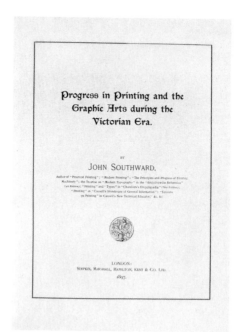

FIG. 9
Jones was a vanguard user of the
Linotype machine for composing
commercial work. An early
example can be seen in a book
by John Southward of 1897.

and remained more prominent in that sector of the industry, being
initially less evident in general commercial printing. As a consequence, Jones was a pioneer in more senses than one. It must be
understood, too, that Jones entered the industry in 1872 when handsetting was virtually the sole method of assembling metal type. The
Family Herald publication had flirted with the Pianotyp machine of
Young and Delcambre after 1840, though not on a permanent basis.
Probably the Hattersley device at the *Eastern Morning News* in Hull
during 1866 demonstrated the concepts of mechanical composition
more convincingly, as did the Kastenbein system at *The Times* in
London during 1872. But the Blower Linotype machine of 1886
really pointed the way to the future by casting fresh type from
molten metal, rather than assembling cold pre-cast metal stamps, as
in the Hattersley, Kastenbein and other contraptions.

    The Linotype machine was an ingenious and productive inven-
tion that revolutionised typesetting, but the mechanisms were crude
in certain respects. In essence, the machine assembled (under human

control of a keyboard) a line of matrices and therefrom cast solid slugs or lines of type from molten metal. Afterwards the solidified slugs were rotated past a stationary knife for back planing to paper height and then pushed between two parallel knives for trimming to body size. It will be appreciated, therefore, that the various knives could easily be forced out of true to deliver slugs uneven across a line in type height and body size which necessitated tedious compensations in press make-ready for printing and in manual page make-up. One needed to exercise vigilance in checking the dimensional accuracy of slugs on a routine basis and to instigate corrective mechanical adjustments when required. Jones seems to have understood these constraints and underlying opportunities very well.

Theodore Low De Vinne, the renowned and respected American printer, was another tradesman to appreciate quickly the efficacy of Linotype composition. His company wrote to the Mergenthaler Linotype Co. in New York during 1902 extolling the virtues of the slug system.

Our early doubts of the usefulness of the Linotype machine in a book printing house have been effectually removed. After long experience we are able to say that, in the hands of competent operators, who understand and care for its mechanism, the Linotype produces excellent faces of letter and true bodies of slugs. From these slugs we make electrotype plates that please pressmen as well as electrotypers, and the presswork either from slugs or plates is always satisfactory to our critical customers. We do not speed the machine as fast as is customary in newspaper work, for we look after trifles, but we do get results enough to prove that it is a most valuable acquisition to our house.[3]

It was the perceived wisdom (in Britain at least) that the finest work could only be accomplished on a Monotype system, but Jones proved the exception and argued the case vigorously on occasions. James Shand, of the Shenval Press at Hertford, wrote to him in 1937. 'I do not question the virtues of the slug in the hands of such a craftsman as yourself. But the real problem of the slug machine seems to be in the hands of the ordinary operator' where 'it is more likely to go wrong and provide an inefficient printing surface'.[4]

By March 1900 the Linotype Co. Ltd advertised that *The Printing World* was entirely set by its method. In June of the same year,

Linotype Notes could not resist reference to the development and pointed out that there 'is no sacrifice to the usual excellent style of the journal, and we are given to understand that the saving to Mr. G.W. Jones, the proprietor, has been considerable'. Jones remained a staunch devotee of the Linotype machine right up to retirement. His compositions were beautifully compact and even.

From the earliest time, Jones established strong links with the management of the Linotype organisation in Britain, which were to become even closer. In the July 1899 issue of *The Printing World*, the editorial dealt with 'The Triumph of the Linotype', which constituted an encomium for the slug system of composition and a panegyric to Joseph Lawrence, then Chairman of the company. The reason for the editorial was a newly-published keepsake of the company. Presumably Jones wrote the editorial anonymously and remarked on the clarity of the production. 'We say, without fear of contradiction, that in beauty of "face", in clearness of impression, and in every other detail, the Souvenir must appeal to the educated eye of the experienced printer as possessing all the best attributes of superior printing, with the addition of certain merits that are too rarely seen in even the best hand-setting – notably the remarkably even and equal spacing.'

By the following year, Jones was printing work for the company, including a booklet containing a description of the machine and illustrations of its various parts. The *British and Colonial Printer* observed that the 'text of the booklet was set up on the Linotype machine and printed direct from the bars, the result showing the capacity of the Linotype to produce a face of type that is equal to the finest printing. The printing was done by Mr. Geo. W. Jones . . . in a splendid manner.'

Jones was not averse to complicity in economising on the truth when promoting the Linotype cause, as seen in *The Linotype Record* for January 1922. It was set and printed by him and the inside front cover carried the ensuing statement set in Bodoni.

This Quarterly is an example of modern Linotype Typography, set and printed by a London house which, until a few months ago, had no practical knowledge of Linotype composition. Copy for this issue was sent to the printers with only one instruction: that the entire contents were to be set on their Linotype machine. The October [1921] issue of the journal was

FIG. 10
Jones was a pioneering user of the
Miehle two-revolution cylinder
printing machine, as promoted in
the trade press of the time.

produced under similar conditions. With these facts before him, we ask
every letterpress printer who has not a Linotype, or who has yet to install
modern Linotypes, to examine his copies of this journal and to compare the
typography with similar work in his own office.[5]

By my reckoning Jones had been using Linotype composition for a
quarter of a century when this statement was printed, which
scarcely qualifies as a novice!

MIEHLE

Jones favoured the Miehle machine for printing: a device invented
and first built in America around 1885[6] and 1887.[7] It was initially
imported into the United Kingdom some years later in 1896. The
earliest definitive reference[8] I have traced to Jones using a Miehle
occurred in 1900 when printing a Double Demy sheet (22.5 × 35
inches) of three-colour process illustrations from plates made by

FIG. II
The Arab platen letterpress machine was much admired by Jones. He contributed a testimonial for advertising the device in the trade press.

Carl Hentschel Ltd, with inks from Ault & Wiborg, and on paper from John Galpin, a merchant in Fleet Street. Note that Jones was employing the Miehle machine within five years of its initial importation into Britain.

Prior to the Miehle, printers were obliged to employ stop-cylinder machines (Wharfedales invented in 1858[9]) for producing large sheets of material. In operation, the type bed travelled the length of the machine as the cylinder rotated to make a print. Then the cylinder stopped as the bed completed the return stroke to its starting position. The cylinder embodied a cut-away portion to prevent fouling the type as the bed travelled beneath on the non-printing pass. All the stopping and starting caused vibration and juddering not conducive to finely-registered colour work, whereas the Miehle was a two-revolution machine in which the cylinder rotated continuously. It was in contact with the type for printing and lifted clear for the cylinder to complete a second non-printing revolution as the bed returned homeward. Such a scheme provided a much smoother mechanism sympathetic to producing registered colour work with accuracy. One of the hallmarks of Jones's productions was the firmness, evenness and density of the presswork, which heightened the Linotype composition.

In the May 1898 number of *The Printing World*, the virtues of the Miehle machine were expounded after a representative from the periodical visited the London works of Cassell & Co. under the watchful eyes of the manager F. Hedger, Jones's predecessor as an examiner in typography for the City & Guilds of London Institute. He delegated an anonymous foreman printer to give 'an exhaustive explanation' of the machine which was inspected when running. One overriding observation by the visitor was the 'smoothness of the running and the absence of the noise and jar so common in large printing machinery. This easy movement is effected by means of air buffers for resisting the rebound of the carriage, and by perfect gearing of all important parts.' The article concluded: 'We happen to know that the Miehle is rapidly gaining ground in the country, and that it is a favourite wherever it is known. Many of these machines have been laid down in London and the provinces, and they have everywhere given entire satisfaction. They have been tested in some of the largest houses in the trade, and the best proof of their merits is the fact that these firms invariably give repeat orders.'

One speculates on whether the visit to the Cassell factory was made by Jones, and whether it convinced him to buy a Miehle machine. He appears to have been well-informed on the intricacies of presswork, as seen some years later in the pages of *The British Printer* for August/September 1913 when answering readers' queries on the vexed matter of a yielding cylinder. Incidentally, Cassell & Co. was the first British user of a redesigned Monotype system of composition in 1900, and installed the first three Miehle machines imported to Britain.

Jones's taste in jobbing platen presses was eclectic. He used Armoury and Mitre art machines where the platen made a parallel approach to the type bed (excellent for colour work) under a crank action, as well as clamshell machines with the platen hinged below the type bed as in the Arab and Reddish Jobber models. All these machines have been positively identified with Jones around the years 1894 and 1895, though he had probably employed most of them years before. He wrote knowledgeably in *The British Printer* for June/July 1912 on the subject of 'The Selection of Platen Machines: their mechanical features in relation to speed and wear-and-tear'. George Gordon, an American, invented the first jobbing platen press in 1851 some twenty-one years before Jones came into the trade.

Enough has been said to indicate that Jones was an eager and courageous innovator in the application of new technical methods. He was not shy in telling the trade of his equipment preferences, as testified by various endorsements in suppliers' advertisements. In 1894 he enthusiastically extolled the joys of possessing an Arab platen manufactured by Josiah Wade Ltd of Halifax. 'It is always a pleasure to bear testimony to the excellence of the "Arab" machine. I have now had thirteen years' experience of them, and have four – three Crown Folio and one Foolscap Folio – in regular use on the best classes of work. The mechanism of the machines is simply perfect, and the results obtained from them all that one can desire.'[10] The information given by Jones implies that he first utilised an Arab platen when working in Sheffield.

Some months later in 1894, Jones was bringing to the attention of fellow printers the benefits of the locking-up apparatus provided by W.E. Cook of London. It enabled small pages to be secured in large chases (metal frames) in readiness for the press without the need for great amounts of furniture or spacing material. He was fulsome in recommending the equipment.

Your New Locking-up Apparatus is all you claim for it. Its utility will be seen when I tell you it was all in use within a few hours of being delivered in the office. It is a labour, time, money, and worry saver. The saving of furniture and of time in many jobs is very great, and the risk of accident, as against the use of large quantities of furniture, is reduced to a minimum. It does not spring, is very true and easy to manipulate, and I shall be much surprised if it has not an enormous sale. It will be of advantage in any office, but should be a boon to most of our large printing firms.[11]

Even a modest ink additive received the benediction of Jones in 1894, accompanied by that of Horace Hart, then Controller of the University Press, Oxford. The opinion of Jones on Veseloid by Parsons, Fletcher & Co. was dilated.

I deem it a pleasurable duty to write you in reference to the merits of your 'Veseloid'. Its action on the inks, whilst not interfering with their brilliancy, is to render them soft and clean working; and on rollers generally its effect is to keep them in perfect working condition. What we, however, consider one of its finest features as it affects my own work, is the very great assistance it is in the printing of high-class halftone engravings, especially with letterpress, as you know my people are constantly engaged in this class of work, and 'Veseloid' is one of the chief aids to the fine effect my customers are pleased to say we get.[12]

Somewhat later, in 1919, Jones was complimentary about the stereotype plates made by the Dalziel Foundry Ltd, and the associated colour register system and Parker plate-mounting boards from the same company. The latter were constituted of a wood compound and had a grid scored upon their surface to aid page positioning. They were much more stable and warp-resistant than ordinary wood mounts. Jones's ratification of the system was concise. 'I certify that I have printed several sheets in two colours and in three colours from considerable numbers of DALZIEL STEREOS (as many as forty-eight duplicates on one sheet). These stereos have been mounted in good register on PARKER'S PATENT MOUNTING BOARDS by means of DALZIEL'S PATENT COLOUR REGISTER SYSTEM and have given me most satisfactory results.'[13] It is evident that Jones accomplished high-quality printing with the most up-to-date machines and methods. He did not countenance archaic practices.

CHAPTER 5

Colour Printer

It has been shown that Jones was in the forefront of pioneering the use of Linotype and Miehle machines, as well as other advanced and novel techniques. His attitude to process colour reproduction was imbued with the same spirit of innovation. It was not until 1892 that the first British three-colour letterpress halftone print was issued by Waterlow & Son Ltd,[1] while the process was not established on a sound commercial footing until 1893.[2] *The British Printer* for September/October 1893 carried its first insert by the three-colour letterpress process: a still-life reproduction from blocks made by Husnik & Hausler of Prague. Jones produced a number of poly-chromatic prints for *The Printing World*, but initially they were coloured tint infills of line work, such as an advertisement for his company in the January 1895 issue from blocks made by Garrett & Walsh. Some months later, in April 1895, Jones printed for the same periodical a two-colour halftone from blocks provided by John Swain & Son, reproduced in Art Brown No. 2 and Green Black inks supplied by Parsons, Fletcher & Co.

He seems to have entered wholeheartedly into the production of three-colour process letterpress prints in 1899, with a number of examples adorning *The Printing World* (see colour illustration 3). In the May number a reproduction of a gilt and enamelled Dutch bookbinding of 1589 appeared. Jones printed the supplement on an

COLOUR ILLUSTRATION 1 *(see p31)*
Jones started a business
of his own in London
during 1889. It progressed
rapidly and moved to
more capacious premises.
In 1891 the company could
be found at 35 St Bride Street,
as a colourful piece
of publicity proclaimed.

COLOUR ILLUSTRATION 2 *(see p32)*
The first issue of
The Printing World
magazine, published and
printed by Jones, appeared
in January 1893.

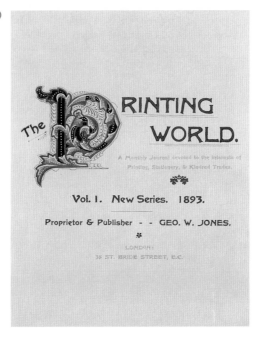

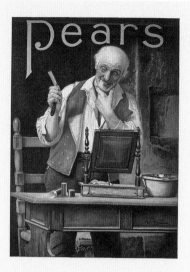

Pears
Specimen of Three-Colour Printing
by GEO. W. JONES, Saint Bride House,
Dean Street, Fetter Lane, London, E.C.

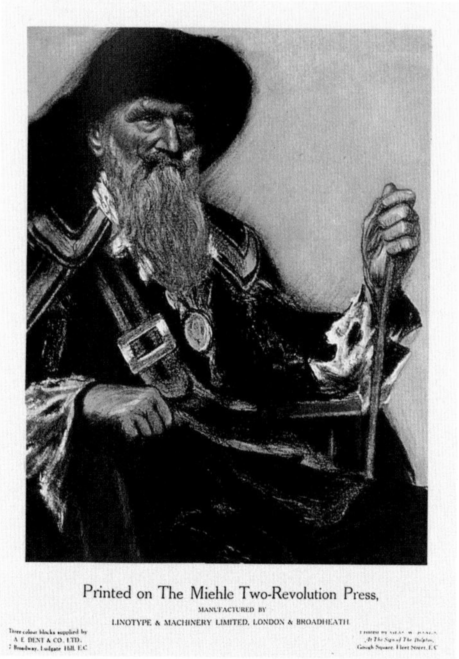
Printed on The Miehle Two-Revolution Press,
MANUFACTURED BY
LINOTYPE & MACHINERY LIMITED, LONDON & BROADHEATH
Three-colour blocks supplied by
A. E. DENT & CO. LTD.,
7 Broadway, Ludgate Hill, E.C.
At The Sign of The Dolphin,
Gough Square, Fleet Street, E.C.

COLOUR ILLUSTRATION 3 *(see p48)*
An early example of trichromatic letterpress printing by Jones that appeared in the trade press.

COLOUR ILLUSTRATION 5 *(see p61)*
The first known reference to the Sign of the Dolphin Press occurred in *Linotype Notes* of 1911.

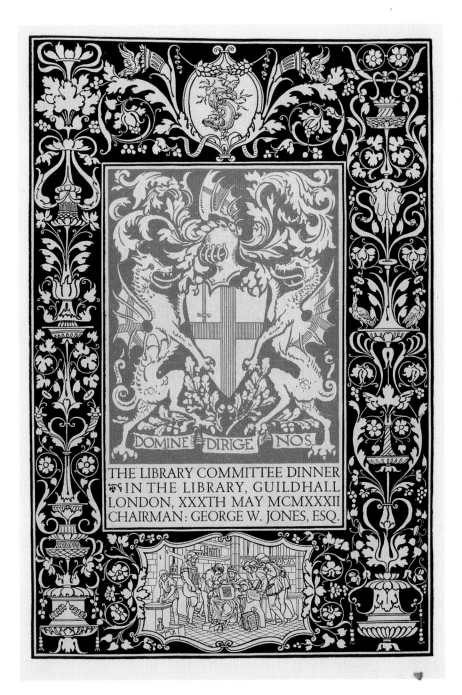

DOMINE DIRIGE NOS.

THE LIBRARY COMMITTEE DINNER
IN THE LIBRARY, GUILDHALL
LONDON, XXXTH MAY MCMXXXII
CHAIRMAN: GEORGE W. JONES, ESQ.

COLOUR ILLUSTRATION 4 (*see p60*)
Jones was a Councillor of the City of London
(elected 1929) and became Chairman of the
Library Committee. This menu was produced by
Jones for a Library Committee Dinner of 1932.

THE GRAND LODGE OF SCOTLAND
ST. ANDREW'S FESTIVAL AND
AFFILIATION OF BROTHER
H.R.H. THE PRINCE OF WALES

FREEMASON HALL
EDINBURGH
XXVII NOVEMBER, MCXIV

COLOUR ILLUSTRATION 6 *(see p62)*
A piece of job printing produced in 1921 and set
in Venezia. Jones excelled at this kind of work.

PEARL: AN ENGLISH POEM OF
THE FOURTEENTH CENTURY
RE-SET IN MODERN ENGLISH
BY ISRAEL GOLLANCZ.

IMPRINTED & PUBLISHED BY GEO.W. JONES
AT THE SIGN OF THE DOLPHIN IN GOUGH
SQUARE, FLEET STREET, LONDON, & SOLD
FOR AND ON BEHALF OF THE BRITISH RED
CROSS. MCMXVIII.

COLOUR ILLUSTRATION 7 *(see p63)*
Jones gained exclusive British
rights to the use of the
Humanistic typeface from
William Dana Orcutt. It was
used for setting *Pearl*, a poem
published by Jones during 1918
in aid of the British Red Cross.

COLOUR ILLUSTRATION 8 *(see p74)*
Opening spread to a booklet
published by Linotype in 1931
to promote the Granjon
typeface.

DEVICE OF ROBERT GRANJON

ROBERT GRAN-
JON: SIXTEENTH
CENTURY TYPE
FOUNDER AND
PRINTER

MERGENTHALER LINOTYPE CO.
BROOKLYN, NEW YORK
1931

OSCAR WILDE
RECOLLECTIONS BY
JEAN PAUL RAYMOND
& CHARLES RICKETTS

THE NONESUCH PRESS
BLOOMSBURY MCMXXXII

COLOUR ILLUSTRATION 9 (*see p104*)
Title page from *Oscar Wilde: Recollections*, set in
Estienne. It was the only Nonesuch Press book
composed on the Linotype machine.

COLOUR ILLUSTRATION 10 (*see p105*) (ABOVE)
Florid title page from *The Canterbury
Tales*, produced for the Limited
Editions Club in 1935.

COLOUR ILLUSTRATION 11 (*see p105*) (BELOW)
A spread from *The Canterbury Tales*,
published in 1935 by the Limited
Editions Club and set in Granjon.

The Canon's Yeoman's Tale

Here begins the Prologue

WHEN St. Cecilia's life had thus been said,
And we had not yet jogged five miles
ahead,
At Boughton-under-Blean, from
farther back,
A man rode up all clothed in clothes of
black,
And under those, of white, a surplice lay.
His hackney, that was all a dapple gray,
Sweated so hard that wonder was to see;
He must have spurred three miles, it seemed to me.
Also, his yeoman's horse was sweating so
It seemed as if the beast could hardly go;
The foam about the breastband frothed up high;
The horse was speckled with it, like a pie.
A folded bag upon his crupper lay;
He carried little clothing, I would say.
All light for summer rode this worthy man,
And in my heart a wonderment began
What he could be. And then I saw his hood
Was all sewn to his cloak, and understood
Through this, when I had turned it in my mind
A while, he was a canon of some kind.
His hat, held by a string, hung down his back,
For more than walk or pace had gone his hack;

He must have spurred along like one gone mad.
A burdock leaf beneath his hood he had,
To stay the sweat, and shield him from the heat.
It was a joy indeed to see him sweat!
His forehead dripped with all that fearful hurry
Like a still with plantain and with pellitory.
And as he came he cried out instantly:
"God save," he said, "this merry company!
I have spurred fast," he told us, "for your sake,
Because of my desire to overtake
And ride with all this pleasant company!"
His yeoman, too, was full of courtesy.
"This morning, sires, and not long ago," he cried,
"Out of your hostelry I saw you ride,
And warned at once my lord and sovereign, too,
Who much desired to ride along with you;
He loves good talk and sport upon the way."
"Friend," said our Host, "God give thee luck, I say,
For warning him! Thy master, it would seem,
Is a good judge, as I may justly deem,
And jolly also, I dare wager you.
Can he not tell a merry tale or two
To cheer this company along the way?"
"Who, sire? My lord? Why, to be sure—yea, yea,
He knows enough of mirth and jollity—
More than enough. Believe it, sir, from me;
And, sir, if ye could know him as I do,
To see how well he works, and shrewdly, too,
In various ways, were wonder for your eyes.
He undertakes full many an enterprise
Which any here would find it hard, no doubt,
Unless they learned of him, to bring about.
And homely though he seem to you that view him,
Ye would have great advantage if ye knew him.

FOUR STAINED GLASS WINDOWS RECENTLY INSTALLED IN THE TYPOGRAPHIC LIBRARY AND MUSEUM
OF THE AMERICAN TYPE FOUNDERS COMPANY, JERSEY CITY, NEW JERSEY, U.S.A.

COLOUR ILLUSTRATION 12 (*see p120*)
A stained-glass window originally erected in the
Library and Museum of the American Type Founders
Co. as a tribute to Jones. It now resides in the vaults of
the Library at Columbia University.

Armory art platen from plates prepared by Carl Hentschel Ltd and with Photochrome inks by Parsons, Fletcher & Co. That was followed in the June number by a three-colour advertisement for Geo. W. Jones, High Class and Commercial Printer and Lithographer using the same Armory press, but deploying Chromotype inks by Parsons, Fletcher & Co. And in the July issue came a reproduction from an illuminated manuscript of the *Georgica et AEneis* of Virgilius Maro, written in about 1400. Again the Armory art platen was employed with plates from the Carl Hentschel Colourtype Co. Ltd and inks from Parsons, Fletcher & Co. All three reproductions were technically remarkable and laudable for the period.

Jones promoted his prowess at colour printing strongly in advertisements. For example, *The Printing World* for May 1901 embodied the following announcement:

COLOUR PRINTING. IN THREE OR MORE COLOURS.
We have unrivalled facilities for the production of Colour Printing of all kinds, and are prepared to give estimates either for furnishing blocks and printing, or for printing from customers' blocks.
Strict personal supervision by the proprietor guaranteed, and the finest materials and machinery employed.

In an advertisement included in *The Printing World* for October 1902, Carl Hentschel urged that 'Printers should Move with the Times and avail themselves of the facilities' of three-colour letterpress printing. He reminded everybody of the competition with the words: 'Why Employ Old-Fashioned Lithography when, on their own letterpress machines, printers may obtain results in three printings that cannot be equalled by any number of runs on Stone?' He had earlier explained in other advertisements that the coloured originals could be 'Oil Paintings, Water Colors, Natural Objects, Old Prints', and so on. Hentschel seemed undecided as to how the word 'colour' should be spelled; he was cavalier about including or excluding the letter 'u'.

In May 1901 the first book in Britain to contain three-colour halftones was published by A. & C. Black Ltd, namely *War Impressions*, with colour drawings by Mortimer Menpes (1860–1938) and text by his daughter Dorothy.[3] The plates were made by Carl

Hentschel Ltd using its much-vaunted Colourtype process and printed by George W. Jones Ltd.[4] Ninety-nine full-page colour illustrations were included in the book, which ran to 3,000 copies. The volume was an immediate success (reprinting in 1903) and became the forerunner of the Twenty Shilling Series of books in a uniform format distributed by the publishers. Indeed the series ran to ninety-two titles.[5] R. & R. Clark printed the text for this title and most others in the series. The colour reproductions in the first and subsequent volumes have been described as 'of a quality rarely matched in three-colour illustration since that time'.[6] Jones's second library, assembled in his office at Gough Square in London, contained many presentation and autographed copies from the Black colour series of books, which testifies to his substantial contribution to the realisation of this resoundingly successful publishing venture.

Jones claimed that the 'colour work of nearly the whole of these books' was printed by his company.[7] My persuasion is that he was actively involved with the production of A. & C. Black colour books up to the middle of 1908 and perhaps sporadically after the middle of 1911. Other early titles that were indisputably illustrated with colour prints by Jones[8] include: *Japan* (1901), *Egypt* (1902), *The Holy Land* (1902), *The Channel Islands* (1904), *Abbotsford* (1905), *Burma* (1905), *Kate Greenaway* (1905), *Birket Foster* (1906), *Constantinople* (1906), *The Highlands and Islands of Scotland* (1906), and *The Thames* (1906). In addition, any book bearing the imprint of the Menpes Press is attributable to Jones up to the year 1908, but not afterwards. The illustrations were printed in sheets of eight to view.[9] In the case of the *Birket Foster* volume, the colour printing was shared with the firm of Edmund Evans, the principal of which died in 1905.

Jones paraded, in his own advertisements, extracts from some of the reviews of the Black colour books. The *Birket Foster* volume seems to have generated a great deal of enthusiasm. *The British Weekly* noticed that the pictures were 'exquisitely reproduced; we only wish more of our old favourites could have been included'. Just as impressed was the *St James's Gazette*, which felt that this particular title 'should be among the most popular of the series, containing as it does many delightful reproductions of the artist's water-colour drawings'. Arguably more excited was the *Morning Leader*, remarking that the 'illustrations are the great attraction of this handsome volume. In many instances there is almost the sharpness of outline of a Baxter print.'

Burma was another title with colour reproductions by Jones that elicited much acclaim. The *Liverpool Post* extolled the work as 'bright to read and beautiful to look at, and is worth possessing if only as an illustration of the perfection to which the craft of printing in colours has been brought'. No less flattering was the review in the *Daily Chronicle,* which commended the publisher for the 'reproduction of . . . delicately delightful colouring in a series of illustrations which are simply extraordinary as suggestions of the tone and atmosphere of Burmese life'.

Following a lecture on three-colour printing by Harvey Dalziel in 1903 which had been critical of printers, Carl Hentschel cited a number of competently-produced books that should be exempt from the opprobrium. He noted *World Pictures*, *Japan* and *Egypt* in the A. & C. Black series. Jones's work on the latter was described as a 'highly meritorious performance, in which the crude elementary colours could not be separately identified in the finished picture'. He did not, however, say that chromo-lithography would cease to exist. Jones was in the same audience and contributed to the discussion. He challenged the assertion of Dalziel that the trichromatic letterpress process could not compete with lithography and insisted that 'some were doing so to the satisfaction of their customers'. He continued that 'eight or nine years ago, he was convinced that three-colour work had come to stay'.[10] This suggests that Jones was convinced of the practicability of the process around 1894.

Soon after 1901, Mortimer Menpes joined Jones's business as Art Director and colour printing became an increasingly important source of revenue. Expansion occurred as photo-engraving facilities were incorporated around 1905. In addition to illustrated books, the firm diversified into reproduction prints for framing under the brand label of the Menpes Series of Great Masters, published by A. & C. Black Ltd. Critical acclaim for this collection of prints was widespread. P.G. Konody, writing in *The Observer*, noted a 'series of reproductions in colour that stand unrivalled for sheer excellence'. Contributing to *The Queen*, Wilfred Meynell felt that perhaps 'no colour reproduction has ever so faithfully rendered the luminous softness and mellowed tones of old paintings, or given with such a degree of illusion the very brush marks, the cracks, and skin of paint and texture of the canvas'. An anonymous reviewer in the *Pall Mall Gazette* wrote of the pleasure 'to see that such fine reproductions in colour from the greatest paintings of the world can be produced with such exquisite skill'. The *Daily Chronicle* lauded 'a giant stride in the art of colour printing', while the *Illustrated London News* claimed that 'the "Menpes Series" is the best that has ever been accomplished in the way of printed copies of great pictures'. Equally impressed was the *Daily News,* with the view that the series constituted 'admirable colour reproductions of master works'.

By using the trichromatic letterpress process for producing the Menpes Series of Great Masters, Jones was thwarting traditional printing practice, as a reviewer in 1907 explained when generally discussing colour reproductions of paintings for framing. 'In England this class of work has been entirely confined to photogravure and a very few collotypes; until quite recently the Menpes Series of Great Masters was placed on exhibition and sale. Of course, these were the work of George W. Jones Ltd. with whom Mr. Mortimer Menpes threw in his lot as a photoengraver some time ago.'[11]

As commercial activity picked up, the pressures on factory space mounted. In May 1906, a press advertisement promoting the trade services of George W. Jones Ltd indicated premises in London and Watford.[12] In 1907 the Dean Street premises of 7,236 square feet were offered at auction.[13] My belief is that the entire business was moved to Whippendell Road in Watford late in 1906 or early in 1907 and the London address shut; Jones lived close to Watford at Elstree. By 1908, the business was known variously as George W. Jones Ltd, the Cassiobury Press (named after a nearby park in Watford), and the Menpes Press. No fewer than fourteen Miehle machines were operating at the Watford plant in 1908.[14] By 1909, the battery of Miehles had multiplied to twenty, accompanied by twenty-five platens.[15] Owing to the advanced nature of the plant and processes in the Watford factory, a fair amount of interest and curiosity was stimulated outside, as evidenced on 12 June 1909 when a party from the Junior Institution of Engineers visited under the vigilant presence of W.S. Wilson, the Works Manager. The guests were taken on 'a tour of the works, beginning with the power station and visiting successively the studio, the etching room, the machine room, the

GEO.W. JONES, Ltd.

Telephone:
No. 276 HOLBORN.

Telegrams:
"TYPOTHETAE, LONDON."
"TYPOTHETAE, WATFORD."

Photo-Engravers

BY

Three-Colour

Half-tone & Line

PROCESSES

ALL ORDERS
TREATED WITH
SECRECY
AND
PUNCTUALITY.

to the Trade.

ESTIMATES
GIVEN BY
RETURN OF POST.

Whippendell Road, WATFORD,

And SAINT BRIDE HOUSE, DEAN STREET, FETTER LANE, E.C.

FIG. 12
With commercial expansion driven by colour printing, Jones opened new premises in Watford, as advertised during May 1906. Shortly afterwards, the London factory was closed. This marked the embryonic beginnings of the mighty Sun Engraving enterprise.

composing room, the stereotyping foundry, the storeroom, the ware-room [sic.], the folding department, and the bindery'.[16]

Jones's interest and skill in colour printing did not falter for the rest of his professional life. He used the technique on occasions to promote his business, as testified by a calendar for 1902 comprising a reproduction of an engraving by Bartolozzi entitled 'Jupiter and Calista'. It was favourably reviewed in the *British and Colonial Printer and Stationer* for the 'excellence of finish and accuracy of presswork'. Furthermore, the picture being by the three-colour letterpress process represented 'an excellent example of what can be done by that method when worked by competent hands'.

In 1901 and 1902 Jones printed a series of *Famous Pictures of the World* for C. Arthur Pearson Ltd of Henrietta Street in London. The first and second parts of the portfolio had appeared early in 1902. *The Printing World* in February of that year encompassed a description of the work. 'Each part comprised nine pictures, lightly pasted on a demy folio blank sheet, with a tissue-paper fly-leaf on which is printed the title of the work, the artist's name, etc. There is also some excellent introductory matter, written by an art expert, giving short biographies of the painters. Thus the pictures may either be preserved in book form or detached without injury, by damping the back of the mount. Any one of them would be an ornament in any home.' Pictures by Millais, Titian, Burne-Jones, Murillo, Landseer, and Turner, among others, were included in the series. Jones's periodical carried a review of the collection, which ended somewhat defiantly. 'It remains to be added that the pictures are printed by the three-colour process at *The Printing World* office, under the supervision of the proprietor. We need make no apology for obtruding this statement. Our imprint is on the work that he may run that readeth it, and we are not ashamed to see it there. To ignore it would be mere affectation.'[17] Eventually the portfolio bulked to six parts and contained fifty-four pictures.

In 1906 Jones printed *The First Century of English Porcelain* by W. Moore Binns for the publishers Hurst & Blackett Ltd.[18] It is an early example of the skill exercised by Jones in reproducing ceramic objects which was to be repeated several times over the years. He was a collector of porcelain, which must have intensified his satisfaction and pleasure with this kind of work. Indeed a few of his possessions were illustrated in the volume by W. Moore Binns and acknowledgements made: 'To Mr. Geo. W. Jones, of The Grange, Elstree, Herts. for permission to illustrate several interesting specimens from his collection.' In the January 1906 number of *The Printing World*, Jones indulged his three passions for Worcestershire, porcelain and printing by reproducing a vase with the title of *A Bit of Old Worcester*. This colour insert must constitute one of the earliest forays by Jones into the reproduction of ceramics 'direct from the Vase'.[19]

Jones claims to have printed at Watford[20] the *Catalogue of the Richard Bennett Collection of Chinese Porcelains* issued by Gorer of New Bond Street in 1910, an intriguing statement because he had withdrawn from his old firm some eighteen months previously. It could be that Jones was retained as a consultant on the project or that the work had been in progress prior to his departure. Other volumes embodying colour reproductions of porcelain by Jones and issued by Gorer were: *Une Collection D'Anciennes Porcelaines de Chine et Pierres Durer* of 1912 and *Collection of Old Chinese Porcelains* formed by George R. Davies of 1913. In 1928 Jones produced the illustrations for *English Delft Pottery* by Major R.G. Mundy, with text printed by Butler & Tanner Ltd and published by Herbert Jenkins Ltd. Perhaps the culmination of Jones's colour printing of ceramic objects is to be seen in *The Leonard Gow Collection of Chinese Porcelain* of 1931, edited by R.L. Hobson. It includes eighty-five plates, the majority in colour, and the run was 300 copies, distributed by Quaritch. Gow was a keen and wealthy collector of porcelain from Glasgow. Ian Rogerson has perceptively remarked that the 'magnificence of the book was such that it was priced at twenty-five guineas, a figure approximately equivalent to £1,750 in 1992'.[21] Contemporary magazines were unanimously respectful of the book. *The Burlington Magazine* adjudged the plates to be 'of splendid quality', while *The Connoisseur* thought the book 'a delight', the illustrations 'serve admirably to recall the rich beauty of the originals', and the production was seen as 'proof of the great advance that has been made of late in colour process reproduction'. Paying tribute to Jones on his eightieth birthday in 1940, Leonard Jay (then Head of the Birmingham School of Printing) attempted to identify his greatest attainments.

To single out which was his finest achievement is extremely difficult, for I have never seen a bad piece of work bearing the Dolphin Imprint, and I have a good collection in my possession. Two books stand out in my mind. First the *Catalogue of the Leonard Gow Collection of Chinese Porcelain*. This is a magnificent production, and all through I can see the loving care which has been bestowed upon it in every detail – typesetting, arrangement, proportions, margins, decorations, single and multi-colour illustrations, all superbly printed – a real feast for an understanding and appreciative printer.[22]

For the record, the second book chosen by Jay was *The Canterbury Tales* by Geoffrey Chaucer, printed for the Limited Editions Club in 1934.

Jones's precocious adeptness at reproducing colour paintings has already been noted. In 1906 he was involved with the production of *Stories of the Italian Artists from Visari*, published by Chatto &

Windus. It was a co-operative effort, with text printed by Ballantyne, Hanson & Co. Ltd of Edinburgh, illustrated by twenty-four monochrome halftones by Edmund Evans and by twelve quadrichromatic halftones by Geo. W. Jones Ltd. It was extensively reviewed in *The Printing World* of March 1907, which reproduced some of the pictures.

In the period prior to the First World War, Jones printed a number of books for Chatto & Windus. They all embraced colour illustrations, as evidenced by *Artists of the Italian Renaissance*, translated from the Chroniclers and arranged by E.L. Seeley of 1907; *The Colour of London* by W.J. Loftie, with illustrations by Yoshio Markino and an introduction by M.H. Spielmann of 1907; and *The Colour of Paris* by Messieurs les Académiciens Goncourt, under the general editorship of M. Lucien Descaves and with illustrations by Yoshio Markino of 1908.

CHAPTER 6

Industrial Exile

By the middle of 1908, Jones had resigned from his company at Watford. He was quite definitely with the firm in the early autumn of 1907 when he received a presentation to mark his silver wedding anniversary. The gift consisted of three large silver fruit dishes 'subscribed for by about 200 workpeople'.[1] On this occasion George Mortimer made a speech in appreciation of Jones's work in developing the firm. Jones also joined the annual outing of *The Printing World* to Brighton earlier in the year.[2] Significantly, he did not attend the Menpes Press Sports Day at Watford in July 1908, whereas previously he had put in an appearance at this event.[3]

Only *The Printing Art* seems to have commented on the affair, through the pen of George Mortimer, and then retrospectively.[4]

Mr. Jones removed the entire plant to Watford against his better judgement; he considered it a mistake to abandon entirely the London office. He recognised that in printing – and especially in trade printing – time is the essence of the contract. If the work is carried into the country, the printer cannot always count upon delivering the goods on time. Mr. Jones struggled doggedly under the new conditions for a time, but at last he was compelled to withdraw from associations with which he had no affinity. By agreement with his partners, he bound himself not to engage in the industry for three years. This, to a man loving his craft as Mr. Jones loves printing, must have been the 'unkindest cut of all', but he bore his fate stoically.

FIG. 13
Jones in Masonic regalia. He rose to quite a high
level in the Brotherhood.

Fettered in one direction, he broke out in others. He could not brook inaction, but plunged into a variety of activities.

One can only speculate on the circumstances that caused Jones to resign from the company. His earlier history suggests that a genuine and principled disagreement could have been at the root of the trouble. Perhaps the disagreement occurred with Mortimer Menpes, as the two men came from vastly different backgrounds and disciplines and had divergent temperaments. Ian Rogerson has expressed the view that 'It is difficult to see that there could have been a lasting relationship between Jones, the competent professional, and Menpes, the boastful, larger than life "painter, etcher and raconteur",[5] who claimed to have revived "the art of etching in colour".'[6]

By a series of commercial transactions, the factory and plant of the Menpes Printing and Engraving Co. Ltd devolved in 1918 to André, Sleigh & Anglo Ltd and became known as the Sun Engraving Co. Ltd. Little more need be said about the contributions of Jones to the advance of colour printing and process engraving in Britain.

While in exile, Jones did not lose touch with friends, associates and non-commercial pursuits in the industry. In 1899 he had been appointed Examiner in Typography for the City & Guilds of London Institute. From 1904 he served sporadically on the Board of Governors of the St Bride Foundation Institute and on the Advisory Committee of the St Bride Foundation Printing School. He was active in the Institute of Printers and served as a juror for the Printing Section of the Franco-British Exhibition in 1908.[7] On 8 June 1909, Jones was elected a Freeman and Liveryman of the Worshipful Company of Stationers. He was also an active Freemason and engaged in many charitable trade functions, such as the Printers' Pension Corporation. In 1910 he was noted in the trade press as Secretary of the London Printing Machine Overseers' Benevolent Association.[8]

With freedom from daily commercial responsibilities, Jones indulged in more frivolous and lighter activities. He became a member of Ye Societie of Ye Falconers in 1907. William Brett Plummer of the photo-engraving firm John Swain & Son Ltd was the founder. It was a 'social society among members of the printing and kindred trades' which met at the Falcon Tavern in Gough Square off Fleet Street. He was also a Trustee of the City of London Printers' Musical Society, as reported in 1910.[9] Time did not drag for Jones while in exile from the printing trade!

Some years later, in 1923, Jones was elected a Common Councillor of the City of London. *The British Printer* reported: 'Mr. Geo. W. Jones, the noted printer craftsman of Gough Square, Fleet Street, was elected a Common Councillor of the City of London on Tuesday, May 29. Mr. Jones's votes totalled over 100 per cent more than the combined polls of the other candidates. It may seem strange that the Ward of Farringdon Without, which includes Fleet Street and the surrounding district, has not hitherto had a printer as its representative on the Council of the City of London.'[10] He subsequently became Chairman of the Library Committee for the City of London, a sensible appointment given his interest in books (see colour illustration 4). Another position held in later years was President of the City Livery Club.

CHAPTER 7

At the Sign of the Dolphin

By the middle of 1911, Jones had returned as a master printer. The earliest reference traced takes the form of a three-colour print in *Linotype Notes* of July 1911 and bears the imprint 'At the Sign of the Dolphin', a title never used before as far as I can determine (see colour illustration 5).[1] At the age of fifty-one, Jones was embarking on the most glittering stage of his illustrious career. Confirming the comeback, a Christmas card was acknowledged in the trade press of January 1912.[2] It seemed to be on time! The Dolphin premises were located in Gough Square off Fleet Street, adjacent to the house in which Dr Samuel Johnson compiled his *Dictionary of the English Language*, published in 1755.

About two years after the start-up in Gough Square, Jones decided to develop a new typeface exclusive to his press. His paradigm was probably William Morris, who had created the Golden (1890), Troy (1891), and Chaucer (1892) types for use restricted to his Kelmscott Press.[3] Morris commissioned the handcut punches from Edward Prince, and the design of the Golden type was founded on prototypes by Nicolas Jenson dating from fifteenth-century Venice. When Jones embarked on his project around 1913/14, he too retained Edward Prince to cut the punches and based his design on a Jenson precedent found in Caesar's *Commentaries* of 1470.[4]

Venezia was the name chosen for Jones's type. It was cast for handsetting by P.M. Shanks & Sons Ltd, the typefounders of Red

Lion Square in London. As noted previously, Jones first met Edward Shanks in 1889 at the Grapho Press and the two cemented a warm friendship. When Shanks died in 1927, Jones wrote an appreciation of his life and work. Included was the passage: 'He paid me the great compliment, without consultation, of naming several of his types after my home, or my press, or the street in which I wrought.'[5] One finds in the catalogue of the Shanks foundry the typeface names of Dolphin Old Style, Elstree Old Style, and St Bride Old Style to illustrate the point.[6] It has encouraged more than one unsuspecting researcher to deduce wrongly that Dolphin Old Style was the work of Jones. In the same obituary, Jones acknowledged that: 'He, some years ago, gave me ungrudgingly of his foundry craft knowledge' when casting 'my Venezia roman in several sizes'.

Venezia made its debut in the *Shakespeare Tercentenary Observance* programme, printed at the Sign of the Dolphin in 1916. It received an enthusiastic press review which reminded the readership that Jones was 'a great stickler for detail'.[7] In *The London Mercury* of March 1921, Bernard Newdigate pointed out that: 'His Venezia type claims to be an exact copy of Jenson's roman type, and certainly no better model could be found. Comparison with Jenson's own printing . . . will show divergences from the original; it is perhaps not possible, nor would it be desirable, to get an exact copy of any type by re-cutting.'[8]

In 1926 the Venezia type was made available for Linotype composition and more will be said about this later. Venezia is a good and workmanlike type of its kind and Jones applied the design with impact in a wide range of jobbing printing. To modern eyes, the design may appear somewhat antiquarian, but worse revivals have been perpetrated on the industry!

Some excellent early examples of Jones's use of Venezia for jobbing printing are contained in *The Printing Art* of August 1919; the work ranges over invitation and reminder cards, programmes, menus, letterheadings, and business cards for the City Livery Club, Freemasons' Lodges (see colour illustration 6) and other clients. Other more substantial productions in Venezia include: a prospectus for new buildings of the Grammar School of King Edward the Sixth at Stratford-upon-Avon, issued in 1919; *Ich Dene: some observations on a manuscript of the life and feats of arms of Edward Prince of*

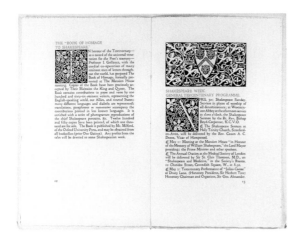

FIG. 14
The first use of the Venezia
typeface developed under
the direction of Jones
occurred in the *Shakespeare
Tercentenary* programme,
printed at the Sign of the
Dolphin in 1916.

Wales, the Black Prince, dated 1921 and comprising twenty pages for
presentation by the University of London to HRH Edward, Prince
of Wales, KG; and *Richard Vincent Sutton: a record of his life together
with extracts from his private paper,* edited by Mildred Isemonger,
dated 1922 and running to 204 pages for private circulation.

Under different circumstances, Jones gained exclusive rights in
Britain to the Humanistic type by William Dana Orcutt of the
Harvard University Press, Cambridge, Massachusetts. The special
arrangement seems to have taken effect towards the end of the First
World War. W.A. Dwiggins, the distinguished American typogra-
pher, did not approve of the design when writing to C.H. Griffith of
the Mergenthaler Linotype Company in New York: 'I don't believe
that you can make a type-letter by copying a pen-letter the way
WDO did.' He also commented on another occasion that 'Old Man
Jones had a grand eye for quality!'[9] Bernard Newdigate, too, cau-
tioned on the use of Humanistic: 'No one will gainsay the beauty of
this letter and its appropriateness for the limited and special pur-
poses which it is meant to serve.' Among the productions printed in
the face by Jones was *Pearl: an English poem of the fourteenth century
re-set in modern English* by Israel Gollancz (see colour illustration 7).
It was published by Jones in 1918 and the 650 copies sold in aid of
the British Red Cross. Another work in Humanistic was a masonic
souvenir printed in 1920 for the Motherland Lodge No. 3861.

CHAPTER 8

Printing Adviser

At the start of the 1920s, the subject of typography was topical. After some thirty years in successful commercial operation and of continuous technical refinement, the mechanisms of the Linotype and Monotype systems had become reliable and efficient and the industry was convinced of their efficacy. Accordingly, the attention of manufacturers turned to endeavours to improve the appearance of the output composition. The advertising campaigns and press relations of the supply houses were concentrated on typography.

Elsewhere, in 1920, the use of typefaces in Government printing was the subject of an investigation by an official Treasury committee which included Jones and other notables such as Joseph Thorp (author of *Printing for Business*) and Lucien Legros (co-author of *Typographical Printing-Surfaces*). Its objectives were 'to select the best faces of types and modes of type display for Government printing, having regard to appearance, ease in reading, and economy'.[1] Not everybody was satisfied with the constitution of the committee, an observer tartly remarking, 'We should have preferred to have seen a larger number of practical master printers on the Committee,'[2] even though Jones was representing the Federation of Master Printers and Allied Trades of the United Kingdom of Great Britain and Ireland, which he joined in 1900. Bernard Newdigate had little doubt about the relevance of the project: 'Government printing in

Utopia is the best that Utopian printers can do . . . in England it is the worst that can be got.'[3]

With customary energy and conscientiousness, Jones printed two booklets to assist the deliberations of the committee: *Suggested Types for Printing Debates* and *Type Faces for Book and Pamphlet Printing*. The latter was of octavo format and bulked to 232 pages; it contained an extensive selection of type specimens from Intertype, Linotype and Monotype, as well as from more than a half-dozen type foundries. By present-day criteria, the quality of many of the typefaces was dubious and uninspiring, but the research pre-dated the great typographical revival programmes of the 1920s and 1930s. Nonetheless, the few trustworthy and sound typefaces available were identified, among others Caslon Old Face, Monotype Plantin (both the Series 110 and 113), Monotype Imprint Old Face, Linotype Scotch Roman, and Jones's Venezia. In 1922, a report of the committee was published.[4] *The Caxton Magazine* greeted the recommendations with a mixture of approval and disapproval. The editorial regretted that the details of the evidence taken by the committee was not published with the names of those interviewed, and that the 'recommendations show a strong leaning towards the fashions which have been adopted by a few workers, rather than the more general lines upon which reforms might be directed'. On a more positive note, the magazine welcomed the common-sense advice contained in the report.

Legible type and clear display is the chief message the report has to give, and the words might be inscribed in letters of gold in every printing office in the country. Not that every job should be set in one of a few prescribed types, and in this or that particular style of display, but merely that the type, whatever its name, should be easy to read and the display plain, and made forcible or delicate according to the requirements of the work. Such a thesis gives sufficiently wide scope for every possible kind of individuality. . . . The Committee has done a valuable service in pointing out that printing may be done economically and at the same time be good . . . To set type that is well designed costs no more than to set in an ugly type, and the correct arrangement of the type on a page as regards the margins costs no more than to do it incorrectly.[5]

In 1920 Frederic W. Goudy was appointed 'art adviser'[6] to the Lanston Monotype Company of Philadelphia.[7] Less obviously significant was

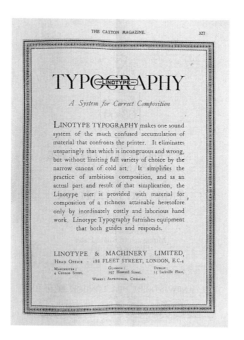

TYP〈LINOTYPE〉APHY

A System for Correct Composition

LINOTYPE TYPOGRAPHY makes one sound system of the much confused accumulation of material that confronts the printer. It eliminates unsparingly that which is incongruous and wrong, but without limiting full variety of choice by the narrow canons of cold art. It simplifies the practice of ambitious composition, and as an actual part and result of that simplication, the Linotype user is provided with material for composition of a richness attainable heretofore only by inordinately costly and laborious hand work. Linotype Typography furnishes equipment that both guides and responds.

LINOTYPE & MACHINERY LIMITED,
HEAD OFFICE - 188 FLEET STREET, LONDON, E.C.4

MANCHESTER / GLASGOW / DUBLIN:
4 Cannon Street. 197 Howard Street. 15 Sackville Place.

WORKS: ALTRINCHAM, CHESHIRE.

FIG. 15
In the 1920s, the matter of type-face design became a priority for the composing machinery manufacturers, as exemplified by this Linotype advertisement in *The Caxton Magazine*.

a visit to the United Kingdom in 1920 by Edward E. Bartlett, the Director of Linotype Typography whose appointment dated from 1914. His remarks about the state of the Linotype typeface library were unflattering. 'It is true that the lino. for America had 1,300 to 1,400 faces, but they did not show enough instances of one good face cast through the whole range of sizes. Further, in the past, some man has easily persuaded the Company to cut certain faces as a condition of his buying so many machines.'[8] His mission to the United Kingdom was to discuss typographical requirements with printers and to determine an outline programme of matrix developments for the future. It is virtually certain (though no definite evidence is to hand) that Bartlett (owner of the Bartlett-Orr Press in New York) met Jones on this trip. After all, Jones had established a reputation as a leading letterpress printer and an expert exponent of quality Linotype setting. My feeling is that the appointment of Jones in September 1921 as 'printing adviser' to Linotype & Machinery Ltd in Britain arose as a direct result of Bartlett's crusade. Apparently, Jones worked four days each week for Linotype from 1921, an arrangement modified to four months a year from February 1937.[9] Somewhat remarkably, Jones was sixty-one years of age on gaining this assignment and seniority does not appear to have been a stumbling block. Stanley Morison (aged thirty-three) joined the Lanston Monotype Corporation as typographical adviser approximately eighteen months later in 1923, and some commentators have sought to stress the confrontational aspects of the Jones/Morison appointments, but the flimsiest of evidence has been summoned to support the notion.

As previously observed in connection with his print design of later years, Jones was something of a traditionalist. His preferred style was limited to the early sixteenth century, both in typefaces employed and in the use of decorative initials and borders. His style was rigid and did not evolve over time or make concessions to fashion, with the consequence that his work has been dismissed as archaic and quaint: an unfairly harsh judgement in my opinion. His efforts in type design not surprisingly evoked the same historical pre-occupations, but as Walter Tracy has written: 'I think his appreciation of classic letter forms was very sound, but not so infatuated that he was reluctant to modify a form where it seemed sensible.' [10] He was an avid collector of books (both antiquarian and modern) and assembled two impressive libraries at the office in Gough Square and at his home, Monkbarns in Northwood.[11] Jones used the older books as points of reference for much of his design work.

One of Jones's first 'advisory' acts seems to have been the establishment of *The Linotype Record*, a quarterly publication dealing with typographical history as well as the more mundane, but essential, matters of machinery applications and maintenance. It first appeared in October 1921 and went on until December 1929. Jones the printer can be seen at his best in the pages of this periodical: the letterpress machining is impeccable and the typesetting attentive to detail. Some of the most persuasive type showings of the twentieth century are contained in this publication. It is sad that *The Linotype Record* has been so completely overshadowed by *The Monotype Recorder*, which underwent restyling in 1922,[12] perhaps to counter its fresh competitor. *The Caxton Magazine* of May 1922 was complimentary about the two external house magazines and mindful of the beneficial influence they might have on printing in general.

Now that machine composition is such an important factor in production, it is interesting to see that both Linotype & Machinery Ltd. and the Lanston Monotype Corporation are taking so strong a position in demonstrating the high quality which can be obtained by the use of the Linotype and Mono-type machines respectively. We place the Linotype first, because their house organ, *The Linotype Record*, was the first to appear in a new 'dress', *The Monotype Recorder* following closely in the same direction, but on different lines. The importance of these innovations cannot easily be over-estimated, for they will react most beneficially upon the quality of work throughout the trade.[13]

Jones exercised a number of typefaces in the run of *The Linotype Record* and demonstrated their practicability and potential with a sureness of touch and aplomb. He indicated clearly that the Lino-type machine could produce the finest of work when handled properly, despite insistence to the contrary by bibliographers, graphic designers and the smart cognoscenti. Included in the edito-rial matter was a series of monographs dealing with printers of note throughout history. Some writers have indicated that these articles were written by Jones, but in the absence of bylines that must remain a matter for conjecture. Certainly Jones possessed the knowledge and necessary bibliographical references and may well have written the articles, but definitive evidence does not exist. Leonard Jay, at the Birmingham School of Printing, subsequently reprinted these texts in a modest octavo edition of 1950.

CHAPTER 9

Type Designer

Arguably the summit of Jones's design achievements was the creation of the Granjon typeface for Linotype setting. It was first shown, as far as I can determine, in the British trade press of December 1924[1] and appeared as a *tour de force* in *The Linotype Records* of January and April 1925. Provenance of the face was in types used for books produced by the Parisian printers Jacques Dupuys in 1554 and Jean Poupy in 1582.[2] Garamond types seem always to be in demand: the American Type Founders Co. had released a version in 1918 and the Lanston Monotype Corporation did something similar in 1922. Neither design had any authentic connection with Claude Garamond, as subsequent research revealed. Ironically, Granjon had nothing to do with its eponymous printer either: the naming of typefaces has been carried out with a cavalier abandon! It was eventually disclosed that Granjon Old Face was a true Garamond derivative, though I doubt that Jones had that precise intention. His unerring eye had simply spotted an indefectible model for a beautiful and practical new typeface.

One of the problems of designing alphabets for the Linotype machine was to produce a decent non-kerning 'f', which Jones did in Granjon with the help of Harry Smith at the Altrincham factory: a man described by Walter Tracy as diffident, nervous and anxious, but with a great sensitivity for letter shapes.[3] Linotype tended to be

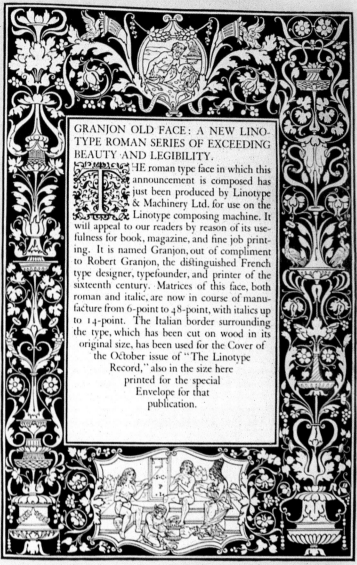

GRANJON OLD FACE: A NEW LINO-TYPE ROMAN SERIES OF EXCEEDING BEAUTY AND LEGIBILITY.

THE roman type face in which this announcement is composed has just been produced by Linotype & Machinery Ltd. for use on the Linotype composing machine. It will appeal to our readers by reason of its usefulness for book, magazine, and fine job printing. It is named Granjon, out of compliment to Robert Granjon, the distinguished French type designer, typefounder, and printer of the sixteenth century. Matrices of this face, both roman and italic, are now in course of manufacture from 6-point to 48-point, with italics up to 14-point. The Italian border surrounding the type, which has been cut on wood in its original size, has been used for the Cover of the October issue of "The Linotype Record," also in the size here printed for the special Envelope for that publication.

FIG. 16
First showing of the Linotype Granjon typeface in *The Caxton Magazine* of December 1924.

self-conscious about the cramped non-kerning 'f', an embarrass-
ment aggravated by competitors from time to time. Beatrice Warde
could not resist comment about 'the unfortunate inability of the
Linotype to cast a kerned "f",[4] and Bernard Newdigate stated that
'the Linotype does not admit of kerned letters'.[5] As early as 1898,
the kern was a talking point. *The Printer and Bookmaker* pronounced
the 'kern is doomed. No matter how much we may mourn the
deformation of the f or j in order to place it on a type-body without
overhanging, we shall have to accept it because it stands in the
way of progress. . . . Some day they [kerns] will drop out of use
altogether, and the word kern, which has scarcely any use outside of
printing, will become obsolete, and be placed in the dictionaries in
small type, and marked "early English".'[6]

Jones produced twenty-six 'f' ligatures for the Granjon founts to
aid elegance in settings. Such a step constituted a two-edged sword.
On the one hand the visual rhythm of the typeface design was
enhanced, but conversely the productive rhythm of the Linotype
operator was interrupted because of the need to find the ligatures on
the keyboard where the matrices could be accommodated in the
storage magazine, or alternatively they had to be manually picked
out of a pi-tray at the side of the machine and inserted into the line
at the assembly box. In either event, the speed of the Linotype operator would be impaired.

Clearly the issue of ligatures in the Granjon founts was a source
of considerable debate and contemplation inside the Linotype
company at the time, though the term 'logotype' was used to
describe the tied characters. C.H. Griffith, Assistant to the President
of the Mergenthaler Linotype Company in America, writing to
Jones on 28 March 1929 on various topics, made reference to
ligatures as follows: 'The "f" logotypes have been an unprecedented
success, and it is really astonishing to note what the average printer
is able to do with them. With a little experience this refining influence can be utilised by the average shop at an expense of only about
five per cent increase in cost of production.'[7] In replying on 29 April
1929, Jones expressed happiness at the references to the ligatures.

Accolades for the Granjon design have come from many quarters. In *The London Mercury* of July 1926, Newdigate said: 'It will be
acknowledged that Mr. Jones and the Linotype Company have

added a very beautiful series to the type faces available for use on the Linotype machine'. Much later in the November 1931 issue of the same journal, Newdigate added that the excellence of Granjon was 'seen best, I think, in the 16-point size, which is approximately that of the *Historia Ecclesiastica de Martyrio Fratrum Ordinis diui Francisci*, an account of the English Franciscans, martyred in Tudor times, printed by Jean Poupy in 1582, which book served largely as a model in the re-cutting of the type'. Paul Beaujon, alias Beatrice Warde, writing in *The Fleuron* of 1926, praised Granjon as:

> . . . immeasurably the best of the modern revivals of this letter . . . It is a fount of light 'colour', and quite delicate in design, but smoothly legible, as it has no features to distract the eye – unless it be the somewhat heavy and wide capitals. These, however, are improved from the originals. . . . There is the inevitable regularisation of weight that comes with any intelligent re-cutting, and the fine M has been misunderstood; but in the main, and for printing-houses who have time to use the supplementary characters [the ligatures], this is a book face worthy to rank with Caslon for usefulness, with Centaur for beauty: sharp enough for publicity, clear enough for a dictionary.

Hugh Williamson deemed Granjon to be 'among the most handsome [faces] of those peculiar to Linotype; the series is particularly admirable in 12-point and above'.[8]

Granjon was also made for handsetting by P.M. Shanks & Sons Ltd, the casts being obtained from Linotype matrices through a special commercial arrangement.

Bernard was designed by Jones to serve as a bold complement to Granjon at about the same time in the 1920s. It was named after Bernard Salamon, the celebrated wood engraver to Jean de Tournes. The reason for using unrelated names for the roman and bold faces

ABCDEFGHIJKLMNOPQRSTUVWXYZ
abcdefghijklmnopqrstuvwxyz
f fa fe ff fi fl fo fr fs ft fu fy f, f. f- ct st QU Qu &
ffa ffe ffi ffl ffo ffr ffs ffy ff, ff. ff-

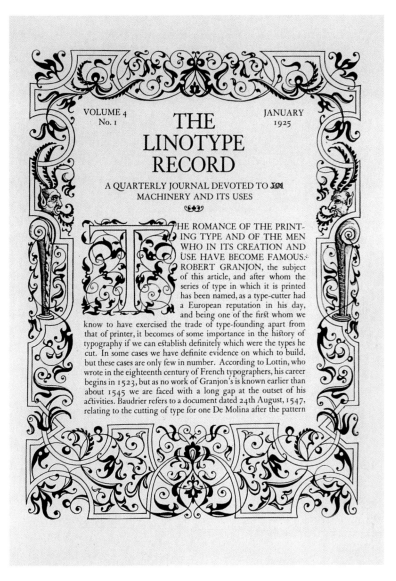

The text within the illustration reads:

VOLUME 4
No. 1

**THE
LINOTYPE
RECORD**

JANUARY
1925

A QUARTERLY JOURNAL DEVOTED TO
MACHINERY AND ITS USES

THE ROMANCE OF THE PRINT-
ING TYPE AND OF THE MEN
WHO IN ITS CREATION AND
USE HAVE BECOME FAMOUS.
ROBERT GRANJON, the subject
of this article, and after whom the
series of type in which it is printed
has been named, as a type-cutter had
a European reputation in his day,
and being one of the first whom we
know to have exercised the trade of type-founding apart from
that of printer, it becomes of some importance in the history of
typography if we can establish definitely which were the types he
cut. In some cases we have definite evidence on which to build,
but these cases are only few in number. According to Lottin, who
wrote in the eighteenth century of French typographers, his career
begins in 1523, but as no work of Granjon's is known earlier than
about 1545 we are faced with a long gap at the outset of his
activities. Baudrier refers to a document dated 24th August, 1547,
relating to the cutting of type for one De Molina after the pattern

FIG. 17 (LEFT)
Synopsis of Granjon characters,
as shown in *The London Mercury*
of July 1926. It includes the
much debated extra ligatures.

FIG. 18 (ABOVE)
A page from *The Linotype
Record* of January 1925,
promoting the Granjon typeface.

was contained in a letter from Jones to Griffith of 15 July 1929. 'I enclose rough experimental proofs of a heavy . . . face which is to be duplexed with Granjon. This I am calling Bernard, as Mr. Pollen and I are both of the opinion that Granjon is too good a face to be mixed up with . . . bold, heavy, wide, &c.'.

Granjon has survived the varying waves of typesetting and printing technology, though the 'thinning' photographic processes and the split ink film of offset printing are deleterious to the face. It was made for phototypesetting in 1976 and for digital imaging some time later.[9] Some measure of the eternal qualities of Granjon can be gauged from its selection for the new signs at the Louvre in Paris.[10]

Jones printed a number of memorable books in Granjon, such as *The Shepheards Calendar* by Edmund Spenser for the Cresset Press in 1930, and *The Canterbury Tales* by Geoffrey Chaucer for the Limited Editions Club in 1934. He also printed a magnificent specimen of the face for the Mergenthaler Linotype Company in 1931. It was in the form of a tall, large-format booklet entitled *Robert Granjon: Sixteenth-Century Typefounder and Printer* (see colour illustration 8). C.H. Griffith sent a copy of this production to George Parker Winship of the Widener Memorial Library in Massachusetts on 4 January 1932. It was accompanied by a letter stating that:

From our point of view, and possibly from your own also, the volume is important as a demonstration of the performance of Linotype Granjon. This face – one of a series of distinguished faces that the Mergenthaler Linotype Company has undertaken to put into the hands of users of machine composition – has been at work for a number of years. It is already familiar to you in magazines, books, and in general printing. In this present instance the printer (who is also the designer of the face) has chosen to put Granjon to the test of austere design – using it in such a way that the essential qualities of the characters themselves are left alone to provide the distinction of the page. In our estimation the type face meets the test: it has, in itself, great distinction and style.

On 28 March 1929, C.H. Griffith wrote to both Jones and A. Hungerford Pollen, Chairman and Managing Director of Linotype & Machinery Ltd in Britain. He assured Jones that 'Granjon continues to gain favour with the American trade and sales are increasing from month to month. This face has proven a greater factor in maintaining and enhancing the prestige of the Linotype for fine printing than any single typographical contribution in the history of the art.' His letter to Pollen gave advance notice of an impending visit to London by William Edwin Rudge, the distinguished American printer based at Mount Vernon just outside New York. Contained in the communication was a paragraph relating to Granjon.

Rudge is unquestionably the best printer in America, and it is interesting to note that he uses the Linotype to a very large extent for his finest work. The reputation that Rudge has established for the Linotype has been influenced to a very great degree by the introduction of Granjon in this country. You will no doubt recall that Rudge was the first printer in America to use the Granjon face, and the fine results he obtained from it laid the foundation for its success over here.

Jones responded on 29 April 1929, explaining that Granjon was a face 'that should never grow old'.

One of the earliest books printed in Granjon by Rudge must have been *The Psalms of David*, published by Washburn & Thomas in 1928. It was designed by Bruce Rogers in a twelvemo format and consisted of 369 pages.[11] It elicited enthusiastic praise from Carl Purington Rollins, Printer to Yale University: 'The book is set in that best of all Linotype faces – perhaps the best of all machine faces – the Granjon type.'[12] In his book *Anatomy of a Typeface*, Alexander Lawson provides some sort of measure for the popularity of the Granjon design on the other side of the Atlantic. He writes: 'The popularity of Granjon as a book type may readily be attested by the statistics provided by that barometer of type use, the American Institute of Graphic Arts' Fifty Books of the Year Exhibition. From 1927 through 1973 Granjon was used in a total of 135 books, whereas from 1923 through 1973 Garamond in all its other versions combined was selected for 148 books.'

CIVILITÉ

The name of Robert Granjon, the French sixteenth-century printer, is also associated with a cursive form of letter known as Civilité. Granjon printed a score or more of books in the design between 1557 and 1562. Originally an attempt to create a distinctively French style of letter founded on a national hand or script,[13] some have described the face as a kind of cursive black letter. Jones had a great partiality for this style of face, as revived by the American Type Founders Co. and M.F. Benton in 1922.[14] He used this rather corrupted re-creation for chapter headings, title pages, and miscellaneous displayed lines often in a second colour. Doubtless the use of Civilité fortified the charges of archaism by his critics.

VENEZIA

Jones made his Venezia type available for Linotype composition in 1925 using the cuttings by Prince as a model. It was announced in *The Linotype Record* of January 1926 with the prediction that 'It will certainly create interest equal to that aroused by Granjon Old Face.' To support the assertion, the next issue of the journal in April 1926 was set in the 14-point size of the face, with the reassurance that other 'sizes are in process of production'. Jones appears to have excelled himself when producing *The Linotype Record* of July 1927, which was again set in Venezia and embodied a magnificent reproduction of a page from the Mainz Psalter of 1457 printed by Fust and Schoeffer. His presswork and setting were immaculate. The Linotype version of an established design was welcomed by Newdigate in *The London Mercury* of July 1926. 'The new "Venezia" is on the whole a very successful rendering of Jenson's beautiful roman type, with such modifications as are necessary to adapt it to Linotype.' Repeating a winning formula, Jones later endowed the founts with a batch of ligatures to aid the rhythm and fluency of the setting. An accompanying italic was commissioned by Jones from Goudy in 1925. Walter Tracy has observed: 'It turned out to be much better than his italic for Italian Old Style – so much so that one wonders if Jones privately improved Goudy's design.'[15]

ESTIENNE

Estienne is a little-known and much underrated design by Jones, the earliest letter drawings dating from 1928 for the 12- and 14-point

THE ARTICLE ON JEAN DE TOURNES
OF LYONS
ONE OF THE MOST
DISTINGUISHED FRENCH TYPOGRAPHERS
OF THE SIXTEENTH CENTURY
HAS BEEN COMPOSED
IN LINOTYPE ESTIENNE OLD FACE
EIGHTEEN-POINT SIZE

SIXTEEN, FOURTEEN AND
TWELVE-POINT SIZES, AND ITALIC
ARE NOW IN
PROCESS OF MANUFACTURE

FIG. 19
A page from *The Linotype Record* of June 1929,
introducing the Estienne typeface.

FIG. 20
Opening spread to a booklet
published by Linotype in 1929 to
promote the Estienne typeface.

sizes.[16] It was employed in the 18-point size for setting *The Linotype Record* of June 1929, a very subdued and chaste issue in the corpus of Jones's work. Editorially, the issue carried a lengthy article on Jean de Tournes, the printer of Lyons during the 1500s. Inspiration for the face is rooted in sixteenth-century French printing, although Hugh Williamson did speculate on its origin. 'Although named after the Estiennes, it is said not to be a direct copy of their types so much as a design in the style of that period. It is, however, very similar to the large roman, almost certainly cut by Garamond, which appears in the preliminary pages of Robert Estienne's Folio Bible of 1532.'[17] The face has a small x-height, long ascenders and descenders, and a blonde colour. In an interview with a journalist in April 1930, Jones explained that he was busy completing the Estienne family.

For a time the type found favour among the better printers in the US, but never enjoyed much currency in Britain. From America, Griffith wrote to Jones on 13 May 1929. 'We are all very much interested in the prospects of your Estienne on this side. The few people to whom we have shown advance proofs are very much taken with it. The beautiful brochure that you prepared for Linotype & Machinery Ltd. is about the finest thing that any of us have seen in connection with the introduction of a new face.' Nearly a month later on 5 June 1929, Jones replied to Griffith. 'I am glad to find that you . . . are pleased with the Estienne face and its first presentation. I have received some quite remarkable letters from leading printers here with regard to it, who, up to now, have been pretty confirmed Monotypers.'

First use of the Estienne design in America was by William Edwin Rudge when printing *The Testament of Beauty: A Poem in Four Books* by Robert Bridges for the Oxford University Press in New York during 1929. On receiving a presentation copy of the volume, Jones was absolutely delighted with the work and felt sufficiently moved to write to Robert Bridges with a request to autograph it. The poet agreed. Not only did Bridges sign the book, but additionally inscribed a special message which Jones interpreted as applicable 'to all workers who love their craft'.[18] It stimulated Jones in 1931 to produce a strange and self-indulgent volume entitled *The Message of one of England's Greatest Poets to a Printer and Printers, especially those who possess love of craft*. The slim quarto volume was set in Estienne and incorporated the facsimile inscriptions of Bridges, together with an extract from *The Testament of Beauty*.

To promote the sale of Estienne, in 1929 Jones printed for the Mergenthaler Linotype Company a tall, slim booklet called *A Distinguished Family of French Printers of the Sixteenth Century Henri and Robert Estienne*. It must rank as one of the loveliest and most effective type specimens of the period. The usual hallmarks of the Sign of the Dolphin are to be observed, notably crisp and uniform machining, close and even setting, an interesting format, and a design appropriate to the subject. Margin rules in a second colour contribute to the attractiveness of the volume.

Jones printed some commendable editions in the Estienne face, exemplified by *The Grand Inquisitor* by F.M. Dostoevsky for Elkin

ONE OF THE MOST IMPORTANT ROMAN TYPE DESIGNS IN

TYPOGRAPHIC HISTORY—THE TRANSITIONAL

Baskerville

JOHN BASKERVILLE 1706-1775

IS FAITHFULLY REVIVED IN THE LINOTYPE REPERTORY

'JUST as there are many "Garamonds" and a notable number of founts which all claim to be derived from Jenson, so are there many "Baskervilles." ' So wrote Bernard Newdigate in the November 1931 issue of *The London Mercury*. He continued: 'The type used in setting the page of *The Deserted Village*, opposite a page printed directly from types cast from original Baskerville matrices, has only lately been cut by the Linotype company, and this is the first public showing in England. It has not received its name merely out of compliment to the famous Birmingham typefounder and printer. It is well known that a great part of Baskerville's punches and types found their way to France; and the faces have been copied very faithfully for the new fount. Baskerville professed his admiration for Caslon's types, although he thought he could improve upon them. Most of us will perhaps agree with Mr. Updike that "his types were not as good as Caslon's." They have lost something of the humanistic inspiration which gives Caslon's types their still-enduring charm. They had, however, very great influence in the development of type forms both in England and the rest of Europe; and the finely executed types cut in the second half of the eighteenth century by Wilson of Glasgow, Isaac Moore and the Frys at Bristol, and Martin in London, derive in great measure from those of Baskerville.'

The specimen setting of Linotype Baskerville referred to in the above paragraph was part of a

12-page inset to the *Mercury* designed and produced by the late George W. Jones, who supervised for Linotype the cutting of the Baskerville face. The object of including the specimen of the original Baskerville types was to demonstrate the fidelity of the Linotype version; parts of the two settings are reproduced by line blocks directly from the specimen, and are shown below so that readers of the MATRIX can judge for themselves just how faithful is the Linotype version (which appears at the left). It is important to remember that Linotype Baskerville is not an 'adaptation' —it is a true *revival*, and many discriminating publishers and typographers have indicated their approval of it.

＊　＊　＊

John Baskerville designed his type face to print on the special hot-pressed paper that he invented, and it will be found that the face looks its best when printed on a paper such as is used for this issue of the LINOTYPE MATRIX; the qualities of the face are diminished when art paper is used.

The present popularity of Baskerville in book printing and general work is in fine with the modern preference for type faces which are unobtrusive in design, round and open in character, smooth and easy to read—qualities for which Baskerville is especially noted.

The five sizes of Baskerville with italic available in the Linotype range are shown below, set on a body one point larger (the text for the specimen settings is part of Baskerville's preface to his edition of *Milton*, which was published in 1758).

In his rise to fame and fortune from humble beginnings, his personal ostentation and his sense of style, Baskerville was a man of contrasts, and even eccentricity—in many ways a typical product of the eighteenth century, that age of commercial enterprise on the one hand and of remarkable fertility in the arts on the other.

It was not until about 1750, when his japanning business had provided Baskerville with a comfortable fortune, that he turned to typefounding and printing—though the publication of Caslon's type specimen in 1734, together with Baskerville's ability and interest in calligraphy, probably provided the impetus for this venture. He spent much time and money on his designs before his first book (the famous *Virgil*) appeared in 1757.

Though we now consider that, in his type and book designing, Baskerville interpreted the spirit of his time, the fact was much less recognized in his own country than on the Continent, where the refinement of his types and the simplicity and precision of his printed work had a marked effect on the typography of the Didots and Bodoni, for example. Fournier wrote of him with approval in his *Manuel Typographique*, but in England Baskerville at first received more scorn than applause.

When, towards the end of his life, he abandoned his efforts and attempted to sell his types in England, he was unsuccessful; most of them were sold after his death to the French writer Beaumarchais. Some years elapsed before such English typefounders as Fry, Wilson, and Martin became properly aware of the virtues of Baskerville's type faces and themselves issued new types closely modelled on Baskerville's design.

| 26 | THE DESERTED VILLAGE | THE DESERTED VILLAGE | 27 |

These round thy bowers their cheerful influence shed,
These were thy charms—but all these charms are fled.
  Sweet smiling village, loveliest of the lawn,
Thy sports are fled, and all thy charms withdrawn;
Amidst thy bowers the tyrant's hand is seen,
And desolation saddens all thy green:

A time there was, ere England's griefs began.
When every rood of ground maintain'd its man;
For him light labour spread her wholesome store,
Just gave what life required, but gave no more:
His best companions, innocence and health;
And his best riches, ignorance of wealth.

LINOTYPE BASKERVILLE WITH ITALIC AND SMALL CAPS

NINE POINT: 9◇47

Amongst the several mechanic Arts that have engaged my attention, there is no one which I have pursued with so much steadiness and pleasure, as that of *Letter-Founding*. Having been an early admirer of the beauty of Letters, I became insensibly desirous of contributing to the perfection of them. I formed to my self Ideas of greater accuracy than had yet appeared, and have endeavoured to produce a *Sett* of *Types* according to what I conceived to be their true proportion ... It is not my desire to print many books; but such only, as are books of Consequence, of intrinsic merit, or established Reputation, and which the public may be pleased to see in an elegant dress, and to purchase

ELEVEN POINT: 11◇176

Amongst the several mechanic Arts that have engaged my attention, there is no one which I have pursued with so much steadiness and pleasure, as that of *Letter-Founding*. Having been an early admirer of the beauty of Letters, I became insensibly desirous of contributing to the perfection of them. I formed to my self Ideas of greater accuracy than had yet appeared, and have endeavoured to produce a *Sett* of *Types* according to what I conceived to be their true proportion ... It is not my desire to print many books; but such only, as are of Consequence, of intrinsic merit, or are of established

EIGHT POINT: 8◇484

Amongst the several mechanic Arts that have engaged my attention, there is no one which I have pursued with so much steadiness and pleasure, as that of *Letter-Founding*. Having been an early admirer of the beauty of Letters, I became insensibly desirous of contributing to the perfection of them. I formed to my self

The Alphabets

ABCDEFGHIJKLMNOPQRS
12345 TUVWXYZ 67890
ABCDEFGHIJKLMNOPQRSTUVWXYZ
abcdefghijklmnopqrstuvwxyz
ABCDEFGHIJKLMNOPQRS
12345 TUVWXYZ 67890
abcdefghijklmnopqrstuvwxyz

Additional sorts available

f fa fe fo fr fs ft fu fy f, f. f ffa ffe ffo
ffr ffs ffu ffy ff, ff. ff-
f fa fe fo fr fs ft fu fy f, f. f-ff ffa ffe ffo
ffr ffs ffu ffy ff, ff. ff-
FA PA TA VA WA YA Va Ve Vo Wa
We Wo Ya Ye Yo　7 N Y

TEN POINT: 10◇477

Amongst the several mechanic Arts that have engaged my attention, there is no one which I have pursued with so much steadiness and pleasure, as that of *Letter-Founding*. Having been an early admirer of the beauty of Letters, I became insensibly desirous of contributing to the perfection of them. I formed to my self Ideas of greater accuracy than had yet appeared, and have endeavoured to produce a *Sett* of *Types* according to what I conceived to be their true proportion ... It is not my desire to print many books; but

TWELVE POINT: 12◇813

Amongst the several mechanic Arts that have engaged my attention, there is no one which I have pursued with so much steadiness and pleasure, as that of *Letter-Founding*. Having been an early admirer of the beauty of Letters, I became insensibly desirous of contributing to the perfection of them. I formed to my self Ideas of greater accuracy than had yet appeared, and have endeavoured to produce a *Sett* of *Types* according to what I conceived to be their true proportion ... It is not my desire to

---

FIG. 21

A page from *Linotype Matrix*, promoting
the Baskerville typeface.

Mathews and Marrot in 1930; *The Odes and Sonnets of Garcilaso de la Vega* for the Aquila Press in 1930; *The Georgics of Vergil,* translated by R.D. Blackmore and published by Jones in 1931; and *The Chimes* by Charles Dickens for the Limited Editions Club in 1931.

BASKERVILLE

Impetus for the development of Baskerville emanated from the Linotype offices in America. Interest in the face had been stimulated by eight books designed by Bruce Rogers, printed at the Harvard University Press and handset in the original Baskerville types acquired from the Fonderie Bertrand of Paris. Among the books were *The Passports Printed by Benjamin Franklin at His Passy Press* (1925) and *Benjamin Franklin's Proposals for the Education of Youth in Pennsylvania* (1927), both produced for the William L. Clements Library in Ann Arbor, Michigan. Another was *The Wedgwood Medallion of Samuel Johnson, A Study in Iconography* by Chauncey Brewster Tinker, a quarto published by the Harvard University Press in 1926.[19] Rogers had previously identified the original Baskerville types from a specimen found on a book stall in Cambridge, England, just after the First World War.

Positive stirring towards the production of a Baskerville type began to occur in the Linotype organisation during the spring of 1929. Correspondence at the highest level started on 26 March 1929, when C.H. Griffith wrote to Norman Dodge, President of the Mergenthaler Linotype Company. He explained that the prototype Baskerville face dated from the eighteenth century and continued:

During the last half century some three or four interpretations of Baskerville have been cut by English, German, and American typefounders, also one by the British Monotype Company, all of which are variations of the original. . . . A number of American authorities, including Rudge, Bruce Rogers, and William Dana Orcutt, prefer Baskerville's original design to any of the adaptations above mentioned.

So far as we know none of Baskerville's original punches, matrices or type are in existence, and if we go to the original source for our design, we shall have to depend upon a printed specimen, the finest of which is Baskerville's *Virgil* which was the first book printed from his types.

As I mentioned to Mr. Walker [of the Linotype company in Britain], it is going to take the highest degree of interpretative skill on the part of the designer to preserve the spirit and feeling of Baskerville's work, and I know of no one who is as capable of securing this result as George W. Jones.

It is curious that Griffith seemed unaware of the existence of Baskerville's artefacts because Frederic Warde, working for the Printing House of William Edwin Rudge, had written on 14 November 1928 to Harry L. Gage of the Mergenthaler Linotype Company, stating that an order for 168 kilograms of Baskerville type had been lodged with Paris and would be passed on to the composing machinery manufacturer when received. Perhaps the communications in a big organisation had broken down: a phenomenon not unknown in modern business!

That oversight appears to have been rectified on 27 March 1929 when Griffith and Rudge met for lunch. Afterwards Griffith communicated with Jones:

Rudge tells me . . . he is quite sure the so-called French Baskerville, which was used in Samuel Johnson's Medallion book, is regarded as the original and was probably cast from Baskerville's matrices. . . .

While there is not a great deal of enthusiasm in some quarters regarding our plans for cutting Baskerville we are, nevertheless, determined to do it and do it at once, because I am personally convinced that Baskerville is coming into its own and within the next ten or twelve months we shall witness a revival which will exceed our expectations.

We are depending upon your advice in relation to Baskerville . . .

Jones appears to have entered the project with his customary ebullience and zest when writing to Griffith on 29 April 1929.

I cabled you immediately on receipt of your letter that I should be most happy to collaborate with Mr. Rudge in the matter of the Baskerville types. I have since got in touch with the French foundry which possesses a number of founts of the original Baskerville punches and matrices, and have ordered a fount in the hope that I may be able to get proofs made while Mr. Rudge is on this side.

I have of course a number of books printed by Baskerville, including the Bible produced by him at Cambridge.

It has been stated[20] that Jones was made aware of Baskerville's original materials in Paris by Stanley Morison, which could have been the case, though the internal correspondence of the Linotype organisation suggests otherwise.

The letter from Jones to Griffith of 29 April 1929 continued with a brief review of the alternative versions of Baskerville.

Stempel's Baskerville is to my mind too great a departure from the original, and like your Garamond has become, by strengthening, more of a display than a book face. Stephenson & Blake's [sic.] Baskerville is Baskerville only in name and has no proper italic. It is not nearly as good as original Caslon or Baskerville.

The Caslon Baskerville also is Baskerville only in name and is one of the poorest faces put out by that foundry, and a libel on the types of the great Birmingham typecutter and printer.

We shall need to modify the italics a good bit because in the smaller sizes they must be duplexed with the roman, and also because some concessions must be made to modern use and need.

Bruce Rogers recently sent me a copy of the Wedgwood Medallion book he printed in 14-point Baskerville, with types from the original matrices.

By 9 May 1929, Jones had secured a fount of Baskerville type from Paris. Victor E. Walker, Deputy Chairman and Managing Director of Linotype & Machinery Ltd in Britain, immediately cabled Griffith with the news. Griffith acknowledged the message on the same day. It was initially planned that the work on Linotype Baskerville should be conducted in the US, but a debate on the matter was started by Griffith in a letter to Walker of 9 May.

We immediately advised you that the punches for this face would be cut in Brooklyn. We are quite willing to have you undertake the work for us, however, if manufacturing conditions at the Works will enable you to do so, and particularly because we should like to have this work done under the direct supervision of Mr. Jones. . . .

Jones, in my opinion, has a finer and more sympathetic understanding of the spirit of Baskerville's types than anyone I know.

On 10 May, Jones wrote to Griffith and attached a page proof set in the Baskerville types that he had obtained from Paris. The subject was part of a page that corresponded to one designed by Bruce

Rogers in the Wedgwood Medallion book for the Harvard University Press, presumably to validate the authenticity of the founts. The correspondence continued with a letter from Griffith to Jones on 13 May: 'Your ideas respecting Baskerville are in accord with our own, although Rudge seemed a bit inclined toward reproducing the British Monotype cutting.' Additionally, Rudge believed the punches should be cut in Britain and that the matrices should be struck in the US.

There seemed to be considerable vacillation as to where the punches and matrices should be manufactured. The US was the choice in a letter of 24 May from Griffith to Jones.

Our Designing and Punch Cutting Departments are somewhat inactive at this time and will continue so for several months. In view of this condition it is our feeling at the moment that Baskerville should be cut over here.

If we decide to cut the punches for Baskerville in Brooklyn, and a decision will be reached within the next fortnight, we shall have to depend upon your co-operation and guidance in many of the important details. There will be very little delay in the progress of the work by reason of our having to submit the proofs to you.

In discussing this proposition with Harry Gage yesterday I expressed the opinion that the various point sizes in the entire series should be patterned after the 14-point which I think all of us will agree is the best design of the lot. The fact that the original Baskerville in the form of loose type is practically unknown to American printers, and in fact to printers in general all over the world, it does not seem that we would run any risk of being criticised on differences in minor points of design in our cutting, as would have been the case in connection with Caslon Old Face.

By 28 May 1929, a decision had been made as to where the Baskerville punches would be made. Victor Walker wrote to Griffith that 'you will be glad to hear it was yesterday definitely decided that the punches will be produced by us at Altrincham, commencing with the 14-point . . . At the present time we are somewhat slack in our Punch-Cutting Department and, in consequence, good progress should be made with this face during the coming six months.' It seems that the matrix-making departments on each side of the Atlantic had spare production capacity, but the presence of Jones in Britain swung the final decision.

According to a letter from Griffith to Jones dated 19 June 1929, an order was placed by the American company for 14-point punches of the Baskerville type from the Linotype factory in Altrincham. One issue that had to be settled was the base alignment to be used for the Baskerville founts. Around 1913 the American Linotype company determined that each size of type was to conform to a fixed standard alignment, thereby enabling different typefaces of a common size to be composed adjacently in a line and to sit uniformly at the base. Misguidedly, the alignments were set too low on the body, which unduly cramped descenders. It was a standard unappreciated by book designers of later years.

As Walter Tracy has observed, Jones 'would have nothing to do with the standard alignments',[21] as evidenced by Granjon, Estienne and Georgian. Apparently, Jones's intention with Baskerville was to put the 14-point on a 16-point body to comply with the American standard alignment and to preserve the proportions of the original design. That would have preordained the use of single-letter matrices and denied duplexing with an italic, a policy that would have reduced commercial opportunities. Seemingly a 15-point body did accommodate duplexing.

Much correspondence passed between the American and British companies deliberating on the matter of alignment. Ultimately a decision was taken on 19 July 1929 when Griffith wrote to the British company that 'in order to cast the 14-point [face] on a 14-point body, we will punch it on 13-point alignment instead of the standard 14-point alignment. Mr. Jones was also advised of this. This is one of the rare cases where the question of design is of greater importance than manufacturing standards.' Jones communicated with the factory at Altrincham on 30 May 1929, stressing that the 'utmost fidelity to the original cutting is essential in all particulars as it affects the letters I am now asking for'.

On 10 June Griffith confirmed in a letter to Walker that 'We are all in agreement that the series can better be cut under the personal supervision of Mr. Jones.' That was not only the consensus of Linotype management in America and Britain, but also of William Edwin Rudge and W.A. Dwiggins. Not everything went smoothly, as a letter from Jones to Griffith indicates on 2 August.

Thank you for your letter with proofs from the punches sent to you from the Altrincham Works. These punches were forwarded to you before I even knew that they were completed. I take it that they were intended only to get your opinion of their suitability of manufacture for stamping in your Works.

Immediately I received matrices from these punches I saw that they were entirely useless. I then had big enlargements made from the proofs, side by side with proofs from the original types, in order to demonstrate to the Works how greatly they had departed from the original. I at once went to Altrincham and put in hand fresh matrices.

By 19 August, the procedures surrounding the production of Baskerville were settling down. Griffith was once again the recipient of a letter from Jones.

I note that the 14-point size is to serve as a model only and not as a master pattern for enlargement and reduction. I am glad to have an assurance of your belief that I shall be able to give you a worthy interpretation of Baskerville. I share your desire that we shall have, with the exception of the French loose type, the one true Baskerville type face.

I note your statement that the French typefounders are offering original Baskerville types to the trade. They will need to make better casting than those supplied to our good friend Rudge, for we have found it exceedingly difficult in many instances to get one perfect type of some of the characters. . . .

Thank you for the copy of Dwiggins's letter with his reference to Baskerville . . . I am pretty confident of satisfying him as well as Rudge and yourself, and I hope also to please the most difficult fellow of the lot, the man whose job it is to produce the face.

Drawings for the Linotype Baskerville are dated 1930 and the first public showing in Britain occurred in *The London Mercury* of November 1931 with a review by Bernard Newdigate. It was illustrated by two specimen pages from *The Deserted Village* by Oliver Goldsmith, the first handset from the original Baskerville casts and the second composed in Linotype Baskerville. The implied challenge was to tell the difference. Linotype insisted in 1950 that: 'It is important to remember that Linotype Baskerville is not an "adaptation" – it is a true revival.'[22]

First use of Linotype Baskerville in the US (the prime target market) was a private edition of *A Christmas Carol* by Charles Dickens, printed by William Edwin Rudge for friends at Christmas in 1930. Design and typography was by Frederic Warde.[23] One American customer was quick to comment on the new typeface, namely Paul Standard, Assistant US Press Representative for the Canadian Pacific Railway Company. He wrote to Griffith on 22 September 1931: 'Just returned from a long absence in the Canadian West I find your interesting pamphlet showing the new Linotype version of Baskerville, a faithful, graceful and highly-competent recutting of a type face which must at last gain the popularity it so well deserves, now that you have made it available for every-day use.'

In 1961 Linotype Baskerville was made as photo-matrices and has been carried over to digital founts. Baskerville Bold and Bold Italic were designed in the US during the 1940s and have nothing to do with Jones.

GEORGIAN

The last major type by Jones was Georgian, the letter drawings for roman with italic originating in 1931 for 10- and 11-point and 1932 for the other sizes. In effect, the face was a distillation of the designs that appeared in the post-Baskerville period of the eighteenth century, particularly the work of Alexander Wilson who owned a type foundry in Scotland. In an unpublished article (perhaps destined for a Linotype journal), Jones wrote: 'I have laid under tribute in my production of Georgian, the fine eighteenth-century lettering of our distinctly British letter-cutters and draughtsmen.'

Jones had great enthusiasm for the Georgian development, which seems to have been delayed for a period to assuage the eagerness of the Americans for the Baskerville. Both typefaces were developed concurrently, though the Baskerville took precedence and was completed sooner. It appears that within the Linotype organisation Georgian was initially called Wilson Old Face, which testifies to the influence in the letters. But in the spring of 1929, Jones mentioned to Griffith that the name was to be changed to Merton after the oldest college of Oxford University. It is not clear when the name Georgian was eventually adopted. Rudge had expressed the view that the type would be 'a most useful letter', according to a letter from Jones to Griffith of 5 June 1929. With characteristic verve, Jones again wrote to Griffith on 19 August acknowledging

A drawing of Stoke Park, Wilts, by Professor A. E. Richardson, R.A.

From his Introduction to Georgian Architecture (Art and Technics Ltd.)

THE LINOTYPE RANGE INCLUDES A TEXT FACE OF EIGHTEENTH-CENTURY CHARACTER

Georgian

PRODUCED BY GEORGE W. JONES, WHOSE NOTE ON THE FACE IS QUOTED HERE

Fourteen point 14◇-943, solid

LET me say at once that my love for the fine Wilson roman type face, on which GEORGIAN has been primarily based, was first excited nearly fifty years ago. This affection has never waned, and when, rather more than thirty years ago, the Marr Type Founding Company of Edinburgh was dispersed and, as I was credibly informed at the time, the matrices of this type face, which had for many years been in the possession of that old foundry, had been purchased and destroyed, I felt that an injustice had been done to the printers' craft. Understanding the reason assigned for their destruction, I still felt as a printer that

Twelve point 12◇-A19 on fourteen-point body

such action was a catastrophe. Years later, when working for the Linotype Company, who at all times generously gave me a completely free hand in type matters, I determined to use the Wilson face as a base and inspiration for what I knew would make a really beautiful, if simple and therefore most suitable and useful, series for fine bookwork, as well as an eminently desirable one for the general work of the printing office, especially where composition in bulk was called for. The Wilson roman especially, and the works of the other typecutters of the eighteenth century, with their peculiarly British characteristics, gave me an urge I was powerless to stifle. In cutting GEORGIAN I have sought, in addition

Eleven point 11◇-A49 on twelve-point body

LET me say at once that my love for the fine Wilson roman type face, on which GEORGIAN has been primarily based, was first excited nearly fifty years ago. This affection never waned, and when, rather more than thirty years ago, the Marr Type Founding Company of Edinburgh was dispersed and, as I was credibly informed at the time, the matrices of this type face, which had for many years been in the possession of that old foundry, had been purchased and destroyed, I felt that an injustice had been done to the printers' craft. Understanding the reason assigned for their destruction, I still felt as a printer that such action was a catastrophe. Years later, when working for the Linotype Company, who at all times gave me a completely free hand in type matters, and inspiration for what I knew would make a really beautiful, if simple and therefore most suitable and useful, series for fine bookwork, as well as an eminently desirable one for the general work of the printing office, especially where composition in bulk was called for. The Wilson roman especially, and the works of the other typecutters of the eighteenth century, with their peculiarly British characteristics, gave me an urge I was powerless to stifle. In cutting GEORGIAN I have sought, in addition to its other features, to make it a more sophisticated type than its principal original, by softening some of the asperities of the several originals, but as far as possible retaining their

Ten point 10◇-A39 on eleven-point body

national characteristics. If, in several of the book faces I have been privileged to produce for use on the Linotype, I have given them a regularity and smoothness wanting in the originals, it must not be thought I have been unable to appreciate their humanness. As Robert Burns, in addition to his own inimitable creative verse, took many of the lyrics of his native Scotland and by ridding them of their uncouthnesses made them suitable for the enjoyment of the people, so I have sought in the types for which I have been responsible, which have been based on the work of the master typecutters of the past, to soften their irregularities, not because I am myself insensible to the beauties of such irregularities and individual feeling, but to render them more appealing and useful for modern service. I have laid under tribute in my production of GEORGIAN roman, the fine eighteenth-century lettering of our distinctly British lettercutters and draughtsmen to be found in the mural tablets in our old churches and cathedrals, and on the memorial stones in our graveyards as well as the finely-drawn lettering of our City Companies' halls and churches. I take this opportunity of not only explaining some of the influences at work in the production of Linotype GEORGIAN, but also of making clear to users of the Linotype how I have been guided, not only in gleaning what I could from the Wilson face and other eighteenth-century types, and combining what I have gathered into one type face, but what has been a general guiding principle in the production of the type faces for which I have been responsible. I well remember when the first proof of GEORGIAN was lying on my desk in Gough

Nine point 9◇-B12 on ten-point body

LET me say at once that my love for the fine Wilson roman type face, on which GEORGIAN has been primarily based, was first excited nearly fifty years ago. This affection has never waned, and when, rather more than thirty years ago, the Marr Type Founding Company of Edinburgh was dispersed and, as I was credibly informed at the time, the matrices of this type face, which had for many years been in the possession of that old foundry, had been purchased and destroyed, I felt that an injustice had been done to the printers' craft. Understanding the reason assigned for their destruction, I still felt as a printer that such action was a catastrophe. Years later, when working for the Linotype Company, who at all times generously gave me a completely free hand in type matters, I determined to use the Wilson face as a base and inspiration for what I knew would make a really beautiful, if simple and therefore most suitable and useful, series for fine bookwork, as well as an eminently desirable one for the general work of the printing office, especially where composition in bulk was called for. The Wilson roman especially, and the works of the other typecutters of the eighteenth century, with their peculiarly British characteristics, gave me an urge I was powerless to stifle. In cutting GEORGIAN I have sought, in addition to its other features, to make it a more sophisticated type than its principal original, by softening some of

This table shows the average number of characters given by the different body sizes in measure from 21 to 30 ems

	8	9	10	11	12	14
21	65	61	55	52	49	46	41
22	68	64	58	55	52	48	22
23	71	67	61	57	54	50	23
24	74	70	64	60	56	53	24
25	77	72	66	62	58	55	25
26	81	75	69	65	61	57	26
27	84	78	71	67	63	59	27
28	87	81	74	70	66	61	28
29	90	84	77	72	68	64	29
30	93	87	80	75	71	66	30

Eight point 8◇-B11 on nine-point body

the asperities of the several originals, but as far as possible retaining their national characteristics. If, in several of the book faces I have been privileged to produce for use on the Linotype, I have given them a regularity and smoothness wanting in the originals, it must not be thought I have been unable to appreciate their humanness. As Robert Burns, in addition to his own inimitable creative verse, took many of the lyrics of his native Scotland and by ridding them of their uncouthness made them suitable for the enjoyment of the people, so I have sought in the types for which I have been responsible, which have been based on the work of the master typecutters of the past, to soften their irregularities, not because I am myself insensible to the beauties of such irregularities and individual feeling, but to render them more appealing and useful for modern service. I have laid under tribute, in my production of GEORGIAN roman, the fine eighteenth-century lettering of our distinctly British lettercutters and draughtsmen to be found in the mural tablets in our old churches and cathedrals, and on the memorial stones in our graveyards as well as the finely drawn lettering of our City Companies' halls and churches. I take this opportunity of not only explaining some of the influences at work in the production of Linotype GEORGIAN, but also of making clear to users of the Linotype how I have been guided, not only in gleaning what I could from the Wilson face and other eighteenth-century types, and combining what I have gathered into one type face, but what has been a general guiding principle in the production of the type faces for which I have been responsible. I well remember when the first

The alphabets of Georgian with Italic and small caps

ABCDEFGHIJKLMNOPQRSTUVWXYZ
12345 abcdefghijklmnopqrstuvwxyz 67890

ABCDEFGHIJKLMNOPQRSTUVWXYZ
ABCDEFGHIJKLMNOPQRSTUVWXYZ
12345 abcdefghijklmnopqrstuvwxyz 67890

Georgian is also duplexed with VICTORIAN, a companion bold

ABCDEFGHIJKLMNOPQRSTUVWXYZ
12345 abcdefghijklmnopqrstuvwxyz 67890

These additional sorts are available in all sizes of Georgian with Italic

ff ffa ffe ffo ffr ffs ft fti ftu fty f, f, f· ff ffa ffe ffo ffr ffs
ffu ffy ff, ff, ff- QU Qu

f, ffa ffe ffo ffr ffs ft fti ftu fty f, f, f· ff ffa ffe ffo ffr ffs
ffu ffy ff, ff, ff- QU Qu

ABCDEGJMNPRTUVXL

The sixteen-point single-letter founts of Georgian and Victorian are not now made

FIG. 22

A page from *Linotype Matrix*,
promoting the Georgian typeface.

the verbal plaudits received from the US on seeing the initial work-ings for Georgian. 'I am glad to see that this is finding favour with you all. I am hoping to give you a great book face. It should be quite useful for best commercial work also. It was a joy to see that Dwig-gins had been so quick to see the success of its italic. The face still calls for some improvement . . . I am desirous of getting a better left-hand serif on the italic capitals.'

Georgian was the subject of one of Bernard Newdigate's Book Production Notes in *The London Mercury*,[24] where he commented that 'the spirit of the famous English typefounders (those of the second half of the eighteenth century) have been well caught'. It is a puzzle that Georgian has fallen into disuse and neglect; the design deserves a better fate. Victorian was cut as a companion bold to Georgian.

DECORATION

Reference has been made several times to the decorative initials and borders used at the Sign of the Dolphin Press. Most of the embell-ishments were historically derivative of Durer, Wynkyn de Worde, and particularly of sixteenth-century sources such as Henri and Robert Estienne, Geofroy Tory, Simon de Colines, Jean de Tournes, Jacques Kerver, and others. Much of the reproductive wood engrav-ing was by Harry Prater,[25] and Jones commissioned original work from contemporary artists for specific jobs, including William Northend and Robert Horne.

Some did not approve of Jones's penchant for decorative initial letters. A.F. Johnson was censorious on the subject. 'Another deter-mined exponent of this archaism was G.W. Jones of the Dolphin Press, who possessed a number of alphabets designed by Robert Horne of Edinburgh, A.A. Turbayne, and other artists.'[26] Jones would probably have met Turbayne (1866–1940) in connection with the A. & C. Black Colour Books, for which the artist conceived many of the bindings. He taught design, too, at the London School of Photoengraving and Lithography.

All the decorative material of the Dolphin Press was acquired in 1938 for the Birmingham School of Printing under Leonard Jay.

FIG. 23
Rough drawings of the Dolphin
Initials, greatly favoured by Jones and
dated 1911–13 (artist unknown).

The purchase was enabled by private finance from Mr Marston
Rudland (a Birmingham businessman and occasional poet) and Mrs
E.A. Rose.

INTERNATIONAL TYPOGRAPHIC COUNCIL

Typographic activity in the 1920s was intense, and one cryptic man-
ifestation was the International Typographic Council. It first met on
20 May 1926 at the Hotel Meurice in Paris, though the originally

intended venue was London, made impossible by the General Strike, although it actually ended nearly a week before the meeting. In reality, the Council was a public relations exercise to promote Linotype typography. In the US, *The Printing Craftsman* explained that the 'International Typographic Council is, in effect, an extension of this function to the Linotype facilities the world over. Through its members the Company and the printing and publishing world at large will be kept in touch with all significant typographic developments.'[27] In the pages of *Ben Franklin and Western Printing*, the viewpoint was similar. 'Now comes a further development which is of far-reaching importance. This is the establishment of an International Typographic Council through which the scope of Linotype Typography becomes world-wide and by which is effected a consolidation of the best typographic influences of Europe and America.'[28]

Those influences included Jones, who was a member of the Council and described erroneously in at least one contemporary periodical as the 'Director of Linotype Typography for Great Britain and Ireland'. He addressed the meeting in his usual high-flown style, reminding everybody of the fine printing traditions of the city of Paris (especially in the sixteenth century) and issuing encomiums to the other members of the Council. They were under the Presidency of Edward E. Bartlett, owner of the Bartlett-Orr Press in New York and Director of Linotype Typography in America from 1914. It was just in advance of the First World War that the typography departments of the great composing machinery manufacturing companies were formed: Linotype in 1913/14 and Monotype at Salfords[29] in 1909/10.

Other members of the Council included Harry L. Gage, Assistant Director of Linotype Typography in America and erstwhile Head of the Department of Printing at the Carnegie Institute of Technology (not in attendance at the 1926 meeting); David Stempel of Schriftgiesserei D. Stempel AG of Frankfurt, a notable type foundry and makers of Linotype matrices; France was represented by Georges Draeger, Managing Director of Draeger Frères, a reputable printing company; and the delegate from Italy was Raffaello Bertieri, owner of the publishing house Bertieri & Vanzetti and of the typographical journal *Il Risorgimento Grafico*. Among the guests attending the 1926 meeting were Charles Peignot of the Deberny & Peignot type foundry. It has to be said that Jones seemed perfectly comfortable and confident on an international stage.

Apart from raising the market consciousness of Linotype typography, I find it difficult to see what the International Typographic Council achieved. In an attempt to provide some illusion of substance, Linotype released six additional typefaces to coincide with the Paris meeting. Somewhat surprisingly, a Linotype version of the Baskerville by Stephenson, Blake & Co. Ltd was included in the group, not to be confused with the identically-named face superintended by Jones some three years later. The other five designs were: an authentically-based Garamond designed by Joseph E. Hill; Cloister Old Style founded on the model of the American Type Founders Co.; Astrée (sometimes called Mazarin) by Robert Girard and Moreau-le-Jeune (a Cochin), obtained from the Deberny & Peignot type foundry; and Narciss by Walter Tiemann, acquired from the Klingspor type foundry.

The second meeting of the Council took place in America during the period of the Fourth Educational Graphic Arts Exposition at the Grand Central Palace in New York from 5–17 September 1927. Jones attended. He sailed on the SS *Majestic*, leaving the United Kingdom on 24 August. Several public sessions of the Council were held in association with the exhibition. On 13 September, Jones gave an address on technical education before the membership of the United Typothetae of America. He stressed the need for careful selection of apprentices, the benefits of exchanging specimens of work, and as always emphasised the imperative of instilling into youngsters 'the great duty they owe to their calling'.[30] It would seem from my researches that this message was never omitted from any lecture delivered by Jones.

CHAPTER 10

Book Collector

Much of the typographic work of Jones was underpinned by two extensive book collections assembled by him at his home in Monkbarns, Northwood, and at his office in Gough Square, London. Leonard Jay has written that the motive for the collections was not 'pride of possession but pride of craft'.[1] He used the books as exemplars for his own work; he learned from their technical and typographical achievements and failures. He was practising the principles and intentions enshrined in *The Printers' International Specimen Exchange* from the early part of his career.

As preparation for retirement, Jones decided to sell the library at Monkbarns in 1936 by means of an auction organised by Sotheby & Co. Two years later he vacated the house completely when entering retirement in Worcestershire. Efforts were made to keep the collection intact, notably by negotiation with the Birmingham Reference Library; sadly a satisfactory agreement could not be reached between the parties. In the event, the Sotheby sale of more than 500 items realised over £6,000 on 1 and 2 July 1936 at the galleries in New Bond Street, London. The Birmingham Reference Library bought 129 lots spread over the two days, spending around £3,000. Three of the most expensive items purchased by H.M. Cashmore, the Librarian in Birmingham, were: *Die geuerlicheiten vnd eins teils der geschichten des loblichen streyt paren vnd hochberumbten helds vnd*

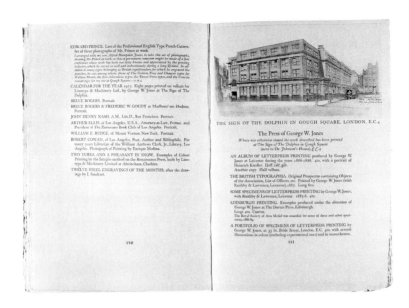

FIG. 24
Jones amassed two significant book
collections. Shown is a spread from
a catalogue that illustrates the Sign
of the Dolphin Press building,
alongside the house of Dr Samuel
Johnson in Gough Square.

Ritters herr Tewrdannckh by Melchior Pfintzing, printed in a black
letter at Nuremberg by Hans Schonsperger around 1517 (£380);
Biblia Latina, Genesis–Psalms, the first of two volumes printed in a
black letter at Strassburg by Heinrich Eggestein around 1469 (£200);
and *Historia naturale, tradotta da Cristoforo Landino* by Pliny, printed
in a roman letter at Venice by Nicolas Jenson in 1476 (£128). On the
second day of the sale, Bruce Rogers wrote to Jones from New York
wishing him well. 'Yesterday and today are the days of your sale at
Sotheby's – I hope the result was handsome – the books certainly are.'

Some measure of the importance of the collection can be inferred
from the introduction to the Sotheby catalogue.

A library of this character has not been offered for sale since the dispersion
of the William Morris Collection in 1898. Like that library, this was
designed to be a guide and inspiration to a working printer and to illustrate

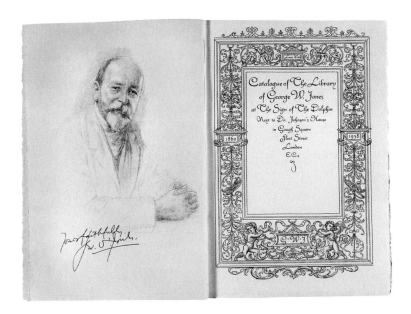

FIG. 25
Frontispiece and title page for the
catalogue of books held at the Sign of
the Dolphin. Civilité is the typeface
employed; it was much admired by
Jones for display lines.

the history of fine printing and all its adjuncts: types, pages, margins,
woodcut and other decoration. The great names of Gutenberg, Fust,
Schoeffer, Zel, Sweynheym and Pannartz, Wendolin of Spier, Jensen,[sic.]
Crantz, Gering and Friburger, and Caxton appear, and there are a number
of examples of the fine borders and initials produced by the Zainers of
Augsburg and Ulm and by Ratdolt of Venice. Notable among the earlier
books are the *Durandus of the R-Printer*, the first book ever printed in
roman type, the *Schatzbehalter* of 1491, the *Hypnerotomachia*, a very large
copy in a sixteenth-century binding, and a copy of *Tewrdannckh* [the
Birmingham purchase] printed on vellum. The wide selection from the
illustrated books of the sixteenth century includes seven different editions
of the Book of Hours illustrated and decorated by Geofroy Tory and fine
examples of the work of Josse Bade and the Estiennes. All the important
modern presses are represented, starting with Baskerville and Bodoni and
including Kelmscott, Doves and Ashendene.[2]

Inappropriately, the catalogue was indifferently printed by Kitchen & Barrett Ltd of north London. Towards the end of 1937, Jones produced his own elegant version of the catalogue set in Linotype Estienne with headings in Civilité and bound in quarter vellum with boards covered in Cockerell marbled paper. Probably only a very few copies of this book were ever produced, but one is to be found at the Birmingham School of Printing. By present-day standards, the contents of the catalogue are enticing and the prices fetched mouth-watering. For example, thirteen volumes of the Ashendene Press went for less than £250; a Baskerville Bible of 1763 realised £10; a complete two volumes of the *Manuale Tipografico* of Bodoni made £58; a set of five volumes of the Bible printed by the Doves Press attracted £42; and the Kelmscott Chaucer brought £155.

R.B. Fishenden, the distinguished trade journalist and editor, reported on the sale for *The Caxton Magazine*.

Since 1921 I have had a number of opportunities to see many of the treasures of the library, including those of the fifteenth and sixteenth centuries. I can recall several great occasions, as for example when the fragment of Gutenberg's Forty-two Line Bible was placed on the shelves. Another wonderful event was when that finest of all books, and one of the most perfect copies in existence, arrived – the *Hypnerotomachia Poliphili*, printed in Venice by Aldus Manutius in 1499. . . . The purchase of the *Tewrdannckh*, printed on vellum, was of equal importance. . . . Other duties prevented my attendance at the sale, but I should like to record a curious coincidence. A friend, Mr. C.H. Perry, who was present on both days, promised to pick out a few items for me, and the selection was left to his discretion to act according to circumstances. He bought three books for me, and I was more than surprised to find that one of these, a sixteenth-century missal with some pages on vellum, was a book which GWJ acquired from me some years ago. Fate seems to have decreed that this volume is to return to my own shelves.[3]

Ending the introduction to the Sotheby catalogue was the statement that 'It will be noted that Mr. Jones has not included in this sale his fine collection of autographed and presentation books', which were housed in the office at Gough Square and were listed in a second catalogue printed by Jones. It embodies the following valedictory colophon:

This is the last work to be printed by me, George W. Jones, at The Sign of The Dolphin, next to Dr. Johnson's House in Gough Square, E.C.4. To my assistants who have in any way helped in its production I give my best thanks. It is finished on this thirty-first day of January, one thousand nine hundred and thirty-eight. For the satisfaction of seeing this last work completed, and for the privilege of serving my craft of a printer for so many years, in the delightful quietude of the old square, just off historic Fleet Street, LAUS DEO.[4]

Undoubtedly, the volume was a testament to the work of Jones. It was not intended as a unified piece of book-making. Instead the various sections were composed in different typefaces by Jones: *Incunabula* in Linotype Estienne; *Europe* in Linotype Venezia; *America* in Linotype Granjon; *Great Britain* in Linotype Georgian; and the *Colophon* in Linotype Victorian. It is interesting that in this work and in other facets of his activities, Jones seems not to have embraced Linotype Baskerville as his own, probably because the project was initiated by the Mergenthaler Linotype Company in America and the design was a fairly slavish copy of the eighteenth-century original.

Sprinkled throughout the 'second catalogue' are some of the most glittering names in twentieth-century printing. Jones had books, often personally inscribed and freely given, from among others the Bartlett-Orr Press, the De Vinne Press, the Grabhorn Press (Ed Grabhorn), the Grolier Club, the Laboratory Press (Porter Garnett), the Limited Editions Club, the Merrymount Press (D.B. Updike), Bruce Rogers, the Press of William Edwin Rudge, the Typophiles of New York, Frederic Warde, the Ashendene Press, Ebenezer Baylis & Son, the Birmingham School of Printing, the Cambridge University Press, the Chiswick Press, the Curwen Press, the Nonesuch Press, and the Oxford University Press.

Leonard Jay wrote in 1942 that the second library was 'in store somewhere in England', and I have no knowledge as to what happened thereafter to the collection. Those volumes from the Limited Editions Club were secured by Sir Charles Hyde, Bt., proprietor of the *Birmingham Post* and *Mail*, for the Birmingham School of Printing. In 1942 the idea of establishing a memorial to George W. Jones at the Birmingham School of Printing was actively pursued by Leonard Jay. He was supported by, among others, Harold G.

Clarke, Joint Managing Director of The Courier Press in Leamington Spa, with a donation of £100. In a letter to Jay of 30 October 1942, he wrote that 'I am an old friend of George W. Jones and have the greatest admiration for his devotion to the craft of Printing. For over fifty years he was an outstanding personality in our craft. I do feel that a Memorial Collection of his work will be an inspiration to your students of printing, but there is no need to remind you that fine exemplars are as important as fine machinery.'⁵

CHAPTER 11

Book Printer

By the 1930s, the customer list of the Sign of the Dolphin Press was impressive. It encompassed various masonic lodges, a number of City of London institutions and associations, the Limited Editions Club, the Cresset Press, the Aquila Press, Linotype & Machinery Ltd, Chatto & Windus, A. & C. Black, H.W. Caslon & Son Ltd, P.M. Shanks & Sons Ltd, and so on. It is impossible to review the entire body of work printed by Jones for two principal reasons. Firstly, the Sign of the Dolphin was a busy commercial press engaged in ephemeral as well as more enduring work, and many examples in the former category have been lost to posterity. Secondly, the sheer volume of work precludes an exhaustive review. Readers would be better served by handling and inspecting the actual pieces of work produced by Jones, such as the fine collection gathered by Ian Rogerson at the Manchester Metropolitan University Library. Additionally, I recommend that readers refer to a catalogue prepared by Ian Rogerson in 1993 for an exhibition of Jones's work, which contains a good deal of interesting bibliographic information. Necessarily, the ensuing review of Jones's bookwork is brief. In 1945 Joseph Thorp mused on the reform of printing at the beginning of the twentieth century and gave high marks to Jones.

Surveying the period with as fair a mind as I can bring to bear on it I cannot resist the conclusion that the dominant factor in the reform of our printing

FIG. 26
Jones in his office at Gough Square.

has been the pressure of the Amateur (from Morris downwards) on the Professional.

The two heroes of the period under review are, for me looking back, B.H. Newdigate, at the Arden Press, and Gerard Meynell, at the Westminster. And I do not see how I can leave out G.W. Jones. If I place him third it is partly because his most distinguished work came later and because though a true Master-printer with a genuine passion for the craft and a scholar's knowledge of its history and practice and moreover perhaps even then the best jobbing printer of the period, his books, possibly influenced by this fact, were exceptional books in which he had a free hand as regards expense.[1]

Jones's printing for Linotype & Machinery Ltd is reasonably well known, but that for the leading type foundries is less so. His friend in Sheffield, John Northend, did a great deal of printing for the type foundry of Stephenson, Blake & Co. Ltd, notably the monumental

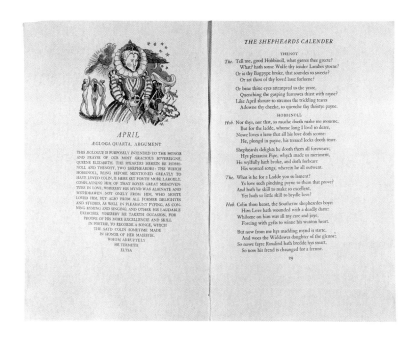

FIG. 27
A spread from *The Shepheards Calendar*,
set in Granjon and published in 1930.

specimen of 1924 designed by R.B. Fishenden. Jones did print a
specimen of the typeface Mazarin for the Sheffield firm in 1926.
Earlier, in 1920, Jones printed *Two Centuries of Typefounding* by John
Findlay McRae for H.W. Caslon & Co. Ltd. It is a lovely example of
letterpress printing in Caslon Old Face, containing a polychromatic
halftone frontispiece, line engravings, a facsimile of William
Caslon's first specimen sheet of 1734, monochrome halftones, two-
colour initial letters, and much else. Strangely, in a review of the
book in *The London Mercury*, Bernard Newdigate attributed the
text mistakenly to Jones.[2] The reviewer in *The Caxton Magazine*
thought the book to be 'a rare example of typography that does
immense credit to both printer and publisher'.[3]

In 1924, Jones printed the exquisite *Caslon Old Face Roman and
Italic* specimen. It was printed on a laid antique paper with an
uncanny evenness of impression. Many of the pages are in two

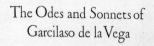

The Odes and Sonnets of
Garcilaso de la Vega

An English verse rendering by
James Cleugh

The Aquila Press
1930

FIG. 28
Title page from *The Odes and
Sonnets of Garcilaso de la Vega*,
produced for the Aquila Press in
1930. It is set in Estienne.

colours, requiring close registration in some cases, particularly of page borders. Some fine-line engravings are included in the volume. Sidney Caslon commissioned this work just prior to his death on 1 November 1923 and Jones acknowledged that 'he made the giving of one's best a delightful task'. The compositor of the 1924 specimen was Bert Smith, who later became a much-admired craftsman at the Curwen Press.[4]

For the Cresset Press, a publishing imprint started by Dennis Cohen in 1927, Jones printed *The Shepheards Calendar* by Edmund Spenser, issued in 1930. It demonstrated the use of 16-point Granjon for the first time, with the 14-point size appearing in support. John Dreyfus has described the book as 'handsome'. Coloured illustrations were provided by John Nash; his full-page drawing and dozen headpieces were stencilled with colour in the pochoir studio of the Curwen Press, though John Dreyfus thought the results 'rather insipid'.[5] Three copies of the book were produced on vellum, with the main edition running to 350 copies on Barcham Green hand-made paper. Cover price for the volume was four guineas – too much for the reviewer of *The Times Literary Supplement*, who gave Jones a vicarious pat on the back but savaged the overall production. 'The actual presswork of the Cresset edition is beautiful. The printer deserves all the praise and the editor (if there was one) the blame.'[6]

Jones printed three books for the Aquila Press, founded in London during 1929 with Winifred Henderson as the Managing Director and James Cleugh, Frederick Hallis and Alex Keiller as Co-Directors. First title produced for this publisher was *Adolphe 20* by John Rodker, published in 1929. It was set in Linotype Bodoni with generous inter-line spacing, not in Jones's usual style, implying that the publisher may have had some influence on the arrangement. Bodoni underwent a general resurgence in the 1920s, especially at the beginning of the decade. It is a difficult face to deploy effectively. Jones printed *The Deserted Village* by Oliver Goldsmith in Bodoni for Linotype & Machinery Ltd during 1921, with facsimile Bewick wood engravings on an unlikely unbleached Arnold paper after the edition of William Bulmer in 1795. Newdigate confessed, 'I do not like the Bodoni character even in Mr. Jones's fine presentment of it.'[7] Reviewed in *The Caxton Magazine*, the booklet by Jones was perceived as 'a distinct milestone in the production of high-class printed matter'.[8]

From the same typesetting in Linotype Estienne, *The Grand Inquisitor* by F.M. Dostoevsky, translated by S.S. Koteliansky and with an introduction by D.H. Lawrence, was produced in 1930 for the Aquila Press and for Elkin Mathews and Marrot. Civilité served for display on the title page, and Kelmscott handmade paper was used for the 300 copies. Plaudits again emanated from *The Times Literary Supplement* for Jones with the words 'an elegant and tasteful piece of book production'.[9]

The third and most impressive book produced for the Aquila Press by the Sign of the Dolphin was *The Odes and Sonnets of Garcilaso de la Vega*: an English verse rendering by James Cleugh. From a typographic standpoint, the most notable feature of the book is the use of Linotype Estienne Old Face for the first time in Britain.

Ten copies were produced on vellum with a prime edition of 250 copies on Dutch mould-made paper, the volume bulked to 100 pages. It ought to be observed at this juncture that Jones printed beautifully on vellum, not the most sympathetic of substrates. Poetry is deceptively difficult to print, especially in determining the position of text on the page with the proper allocation of margins. In *The Odes and Sonnets of Garcilaso de la Vega*, Jones discharged the task expertly. However, the use of Estienne may not have constituted the most felicitous choice of a typeface, despite Jones claiming that an 'artistic-typographer, responsible for the choice of types for the books of a leading firm of New York publishers, has given it as his opinion that every fine book of poems should be printed in Estienne'.[10] That would appear to be a dubious and vulnerable stance to take, particularly as the capitals in the fount stretch to the same height as the ascenders of lower-case characters, making them too emphatic and overbearing for poetry. Each line of poetry tends to begin with a capital, which in a fount like Estienne will unbalance the setting and create a concentration of density down the left-hand edge.

In 1932 Jones had the singular distinction of producing the 'only Nonesuch book designed by FM [Francis Meynell] to be set on a Linotype machine'.[11] The title was *Oscar Wilde: Recollections* by Jean Paul Raymond and Charles Ricketts, the first of the two nominated authors being a fictitious creation of the second. The book was set in Linotype Estienne and ran to an edition of 800 copies on Van Gelder paper with a Nonesuch watermark (see colour illustration 9). That Meynell set only one of the Nonesuch books designed by him on the Linotype system is scarcely surprising. He was a central figure in the coterie of Stanley Morison, along with Herbert and Oliver Simon, Bernard Newdigate, Beatrice Warde, and others. They were committed adherents to single-type composition in the form of the Monotype system, or in extreme and occasional circumstances to handsetting. Jones was virtually a lone exception among fine printers in deploying the Linotype machine to glorious effect and to economic gain. On Jones's copy of the Oscar Wilde book was inscribed 'To Brother Printer, with regards and thanks of the Fidgeter of Types. – Francis Meynell, July 1932'. Ian Rogerson has pointed out that the word 'Brother' probably alludes to the involvement of Jones with freemasonry up to Grand Lodge rank. My belief is that the

'Fidgeter' part of the inscription was a jocular reference to Meynell's endless revisions to typographic compositions, especially title pages.

Two of the handsomest books printed by Jones were commissioned by the Limited Editions Club of New York in the person of George Macy, its irrepressible founder and owner. *The Chimes* by Charles Dickens, with an introduction by Edward Wagenknecht and illustrations by Arthur Rackham, appeared in 1931. Rackham's pen drawings have made the book a target for collectors, though the illustrator was not at his most captivating in this volume. The edition ran to 1,500 copies.

Some would insist that the pinnacle of Jones's achievements in book production can be seen in the two volumes of *The Canterbury Tales* by Geoffrey Chaucer, translated into modern English by Frank Ernest Hill and produced for the Limited Editions Club in 1935. Set in 16-point Linotype Granjon, the work bulked to a total of 672 pages. Three-colour initial letters ushered in the chapters and feint margin rules embellished the edition of 1,500 copies, printed on a slightly greyish Malling Mill paper (see colour illustrations 10 and 11). Every copy was signed by the printer. In *The Monthly Newsletter* of January 1936, prepared for members of the Limited Editions Club, *The Canterbury Tales* was voted the best of twelve offerings distributed in 1935. It won by a gaping margin and not one member least liked the book.

Jones was contracted to produce a third book for the Limited Editions Club, namely *Troilus and Cressida* by Geoffrey Chaucer, which was issued in 1939. Some kind of haggling over the price for the projected work occurred between Macy and Jones. It would appear that Macy unwisely disputed the estimate submitted by the London printer. Jones, an astute businessman as well as an accomplished craftsman, retorted that Macy had described him in the prospectus for the book as 'a very great printer', which implied that the price should have been higher to reflect that exalted status. Anyhow, the book was eventually printed by the Fanfare Press because of the disposal of Jones's company in 1938 to Hunt, Barnard & Co. of Aylesbury. Nonetheless, the book was designed by Jones in Granjon and in a style similar to *The Canterbury Tales*.

On occasions Jones did venture into publishing, as evidenced by *Gilgamesh: a dream of the eternal quest* by Zabelle C. Boyajian of 1924 which was handset in Venezia. Its title page appears in the anthology of *The Typographic Book 1450–1935* by Stanley Morison and Kenneth Day. Filling 110 pages, the book sold for two guineas (£2.10 in decimal currency). An interesting and fulsome review of the volume appeared in *The Caxton Magazine*.

Our readers may not be interested in this literary presentation of the Babylonian epic, but they will be interested in the exquisite way in which it has been presented to its readers. The book is illustrated with a number of Assyrian and Babylonian bas-reliefs, printed in colour, including gold, which add greatly to the charm of the book. . . . The opening page of each act is embellished by the use of a handsome initial and headpiece, recut on wood from some of the original prints taken from the extensive collection of early printed books in the library at The Sign of the Dolphin.

The colour plates are mounted on a dark cover paper, and scattered through the volume to face the text. Their importance justifies this treatment, though some may feel that the dark paper slightly disturbs the beautiful harmony of the production.

Mr. George W. Jones has done many useful things for the printing craft, but they are mostly in branches other than that of book-making.[12]

Another book of verse published by Jones was *The Georgics of Vergil*, translated by R.D. Blackmore with an introduction by R.S. Conway and woodcut illustrations by Edward Carrick. It was issued in 1931. Linotype Estienne in 18-point was employed for composing the verse, with Civilité for some display lines. The edition comprised 500 copies on paper with another seven on vellum. Jones was credited by *The Times Literary Supplement* with bringing to the text 'all the care that a beautiful typography can give it'.[13] Newdigate thought the book 'a handsome reprint' of the Blackmore text.[14] One of the vellum copies was presented by Arthur H. Pollen, of Linotype & Machinery Ltd, to Pope Pius XI.

CHAPTER 12

Jones and the Morison Circle

Some curiosity has been expressed about the relationship (if any) between Jones and Stanley Morison, Typographic Adviser to the Monotype Corporation Ltd and to the Cambridge University Press. Unfortunately any examination is hampered by sparse documentary and anecdotal evidence. One imagines that the first or early meeting between Jones and Morison occurred in the autumn of 1921, an event chronicled by Oliver Simon.[1]

Harold Curwen took me to a meeting of a small group of men to discuss some publicity for the advancement of the cause of good printing. In addition to Curwen and myself, there were present G.W. Jones, Fred Phillips of the Baynard Press, a representative from the Cloister Press and one or two others. I remember little of the discussion except that it became both diffused and heated. The man from the Cloister Press [viz. Stanley Morison], however, spoke throughout with humour and good sense in a most compelling yet likable voice which, coupled with what he had to say, commanded respect.

Herbert Simon made reference to the same meeting and summed up his views on Jones in the ensuing words. 'A veteran was George W. Jones . . . He was a Linotype enthusiast and his work followed – many would say too closely – the Venetian style of early Kelmscott books: the beauty lay in care in composition and perfection of presswork. The Sign of the Dolphin earned high respect.'[2]

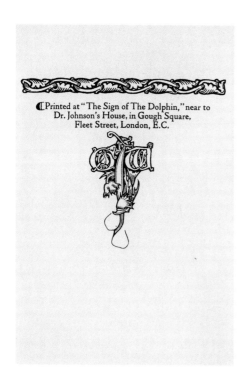

FIG. 29
One of the less appealing printer's
marks used by Jones.

FIG. 30
Aldinesque style of printer's mark
used by Jones.

It seems that the meeting in 1921 did not reach any conclusions and James Moran has speculated that 'possibly Jones, the patriarch, could not see eye to eye with his juniors. Phillips was probably more sympathetic, as later he became part of the Simon–Morison circle, which Jones avoided, or was left out of, according to different points of view.'[3]

One can readily concede that Jones and Morison were divided by genuine disagreements on print design and production. Quite definitely a generation gap separated the protagonists. Morison was born on 6 May 1889,[4] the year Jones came to London to set up his own business. Some twenty-nine years separated the ages of the two men, and their working backgrounds were very different: Jones came through the ranks of the printing industry from apprentice upwards, while Morison entered the industry as a 'trainee' in the offices of *The Imprint* periodical and was never a tradesman in the normally accepted sense. Jones dressed in an old-fashioned way and was a proud man, a touch pompous from time to time, and a printing establishment figure when Morison first met him. Jones's constituency was amongst master printers and fellow tradesmen, whereas Morison was part of a new age of typographers and designers. It seems most likely that the two tolerated each other with politeness, but without too much sympathy. In any event, George Jones never became part of the Morison coterie. One assumes that he was excluded from the Double Crown Club, rather than declined to join, for Jones was a clubman. However, he did attend the twenty-fifth dinner as the guest of Bruce Rogers on 20 March 1930.[5] Sometimes the ostracism of Jones was noticed and criticised in the trade press, as seen in a review of the special printing number of *The Times* of 29 October 1929, which included the statement that 'Mr. George W. Jones would have given added distinction to this number by an article on the modern adaptation of historic typefaces'.[6]

Despite being outside the Morison clan, Jones's judgement with regard to the worth of its activities remained unimpaired. Herbert Simon, recalling subscriptions to *The Fleuron*, wrote: 'After some presentation copies to the Curwen and Simon families it is pleasing to record that George W. Jones was the first actual purchaser. He bought three copies of the de luxe edition and remained a faithful subscriber to all four issues of the journal printed at Plaistow and published from The Office of *The Fleuron*.'[7] His constancy did not waver when the editorship and printing moved to Morison and the Cambridge University Press. When Jones's first book collection was auctioned by Sotheby in 1936, the catalogue shows two sets of *The Fleuron,* each of seven volumes, which fetched £12 and £13 respectively.[8]

Morison was not hesitant in directing barbs at associates and colleagues in correspondence. In a letter to Oliver Simon of 1954, he made the somewhat cryptic aside: 'Of course we can't always go on as we did, guffawing over George W. Jones and other heroes and plagues we come across in the Hyett collection.'[9] Hyett was a traveller or salesman with Waterlow & Sons Ltd. One can only speculate on the cause of the laughter – perhaps archaism in print design or a perceived conservatism in the printing trade at large, or perhaps something else.

Nonetheless Jones seems to have been unaware or dismissive of the antipathy. In 1930 Morison attended the twenty-fifth Annual Dinner of the London Master Printers' Association held in honour of Jones's seventieth birthday. All attendees autographed a commemorative menu for Jones, the signature of Morison appearing next to Walter Lewis (Cambridge University Press) and near to Beatrice Warde and W.J. Beeby (an early associate of Jones). Some years later, in 1938, Jones sent Morison a catalogue, printed at the Sign of the Dolphin, of his second collection of books (not sold by Sotheby). Morison acknowledged the gift in a letter: 'I am most grateful to you for it because the personal nature of the book makes it not only a catalogue of books of typographical interest, but a document of great psychological value.'[10] In the latter statement, I wonder if Morison was hinting at a personal vanity in Jones.

Neither side had a monopoly on prejudice, as the remarks by J.R. Riddell indicate when paying tribute to Jones at another dinner to honour him in 1930. Riddell was representing the traditional and industrial viewpoint that was probably shared by the guest of honour.

George W. Jones required no monument built by hands. His craftsmanship provided a lasting memorial which would endure for ages. He not only knew how to use type, but he had the unique gift of designing type, and – thank goodness – he was one of us – a printer, who had to earn his daily bread by the exercise of his art. So different from many of those who now called themselves typographers, folk who came from the circles where men wore long hair and women were close-cropped and adopted abbreviated skirts, but who knew no more about print than what the next textbook told them.[11]

Affairs have scarcely changed over the years!

CHAPTER 13

Jones the Celebrity

George Jones was a celebrity in the printing trade during his lifetime. That celebrity was marked on more than one occasion by lavish industrial gatherings. On 24 June 1924, at Stationers' Hall in London, a group of 200 people assembled for a dinner to pay tribute to Jones's craft jubilee. He had spent fifty years devoted to the printing craft. Presiding at the dinner was the Rt Hon. Lord Riddell, Chairman of the *News of the World*, aided by Sir Israel Gollancz, Professor of English at King's College in London, and the Rt Hon. C.W. Bowerman MP, erstwhile Secretary of the London Society of Compositors. Some idea of the loyalty inspired by Jones can be deduced from those attending, such as John W. Northend and W.H. Hartley from Sheffield who had known Jones from around 1880 for virtually the whole fifty years. Others at the dinner included Ralph S. Caslon; Henry L. Bullen (Curator of the Typographic Library and Museum of the American Type Founders Co.); Harry Whetton of *The British Printer*; R.B. Fishenden; A.H. Walker of Linotype & Machinery Ltd; Charles W. Gamble of the College of Technology in Manchester; G.H. Palmer, the Keeper of the Library of the Victoria & Albert Museum; J.R. Riddell of the London School of Printing; and many others. Another guest was T.W. George from Associated Newspapers Ltd, recognised by Lord Riddell as the second pupil that Jones ever taught.

Not surprisingly the speeches eulogised Jones. Lord Riddell gave an amusing address, but touched on the essential qualities of the honoured guest.

My friend Jones was one of the first persons to see that it was not essential that a handbill should be an ugly thing. It is as useful, if not more so, if it is a beautiful thing. . . . Mr. Jones is one of those peculiar men with a double quality – I might say a treble quality. He is an artist, a craftsman, and a businessman. I always admire artistic people who make art pay. Mr. Jones has shown us that the highest class of work is capable of commercial success.

Sir Israel Gollancz, Litt.D., made a supporting speech containing the observation:

I notice that the guest of the evening is described in different ways. 'Fifty years in the printing trade', but I am sure it was never to him a trade, and if he has made the practice of his craft pay, it was entirely a secondary consideration to him. With regard to the friendship that binds me to the guest of the evening, it arose through my love of fine books and through my zeal in commemorating those associated, in past centuries, with the production of the greatest books of the world.

C.W. Bowerman continued the tribute in the third speech of the evening and emphasised that he was representing the Jobbing Guild of the London Society of Compositors. He spoke glowingly of the contributions made to the industry by the principal guest.

We do not want to lose Mr. Jones for another fifty years, but when the time comes when Mr. Jones's influence in the printing trade is no longer . . . two words, I am sure, would be found engraved on his heart: Printing Art. No man of modern times has devoted so much, not care, not attention – these are not the proper words – but love to the printing craft as our honoured guest tonight . . . If I could describe Mr. Jones adequately – and it is very difficult for any man to describe him in adequate terms – I would like to suggest these words, to describe him as 'The Prince Among Printers'.

Jones's response was less lofty than usual and consisted of an expression of gratitude to those present with special mention of old friends. He stressed that his work had been conducted under stringent economic conditions.

My job has been in the marketplace, not in the cloister. My job has been to meet the various demands made upon us, to accept new methods when they were good and get the best out of them . . . I know that, of all crafts-men, the printer must never leave off going to school. He must ever be a student. Every day is calling for new methods, for fresh methods, to meet fresh needs. Our craft cannot exist even on the wonderful reputation made centuries ago unless we keep the fire going. A man cannot live in the inti-mate relationship of a great calling like printing without getting a great love for the wonderful business of ours, without its becoming a part of his being, the passion of his life.[1]

Jones was passionate about printing and selfless in upholding its finest traditions. His speech also made reference to his home county of Worcestershire and specifically to floods in the Severn Valley of that year: 1924.

SEVENTIETH BIRTHDAY

To celebrate Jones's seventieth birthday, the twenty-eighth dinner of the London Master Printers' Association was dedicated to him. It was held in the Connaught Rooms off Kingsway. Chairman for the evening was Alfred Langley, President of the Association, who pre-sented Jones with a silver loving cup crafted by Omar Ramsden. All the famous printing family names of the time were represented, exemplified by Harrison, Truscott, Unwin, Hazell, McCorquodale, Bemrose, Waterlow, and many others. Typographic personalities present included Walter Lewis of the Cambridge University Press, Stanley Morison and Beatrice Warde from the Lanston Monotype Corporation, and George Westover from the same firm and later inventor of the Rotofoto system of photographic composition. Some of Jones's long-standing friends made the journey to London, as instanced by John W. Northend of Sheffield. Among trade suppliers present were A.H. Pollen and V.E. Walker from Linotype & Machinery Ltd and R.S. and H.D. Caslon from the famous type foundry. William Maxwell, National President of the Federation of Master Printers, was one of the speakers: a fortuitous choice as a stu-dent of Jones in Edinburgh. Another speaker was W.R. Codling, Controller of His Majesty's Stationery Office.

Even the letters of apology for absence constituted a minor Who's Who and encompassed the King of the Belgians; the Lord Mayor of the City of London, William A. Waterlow; Stanley Baldwin (not Prime Minister in 1930, but a fellow Worcestershire man); George Carter, US Government Printer; Norman Dodge, President of the Mergenthaler Linotype Company; William Edwin Rudge; Lord Riddell; Edward E. Bartlett; W.A. Dwiggins; T.F. Jarrold of the eponymous Norwich printers; and so on.

Jones printed a sumptuous menu for the occasion, the whole set in Linotype Estienne. Centrepiece of the cover was a four-colour initial letter designed by Robert Horne of Edinburgh, surrounded by a decorative border by Geofroy Tory recut on wood from a sixteenth-century original. On the back cover, the Tory border was repeated with a printer's mark of Henri Estienne in the middle. The menu was truly a celebration of the printer's art!

Reports of the dinner were carried in *The Times* and *The Daily Telegraph* of 22 May 1930. *The Times* report was headed 'Printer Laureate', while *The Daily Telegraph* was content with 'A Great Master Printer'. The trade press was equally uninhibited with its praise: *The Caxton Magazine* entitled the story 'Our Printer Laureate'; the *Members' Circular* of the Federation of Master Printers used the heading 'Master and Teacher'; the *Monthly Record* of the London Master Printers' Association went for 'A Great Printer'; and *The British Printer* somewhat unimaginatively chose 'Honour to Mr. Geo. W. Jones'.

Encomiums to Jones flowed from a succession of speakers. Lt Col. R.F. Truscott, OBE, succinctly and accurately recorded Jones's career and was followed by W.R. Codling, CB, CVO, CBE. He reminded the audience that Jones had been a member of the Treasury Committee formed to consider the typographical aspects of Government printing. He continued:

I may say that he hated the Stationery Office and all its ways. Printing to him is an artistic expression of his own personality, and he found it very difficult to conceive of it merely as a very urgent method of communication . . . . His real value to us was that he infected all the members of that Committee with his own passionate love of good printing, and thereby kept them enthusiastically at the practical task of improving the standard. . . . He personally prepared all the specifications, layouts, and pages of type for the Committee.

William Maxwell spoke next as 'one of his old boys' from the Edinburgh training classes.

I have two inspirations – the first is George W. Jones and the second is Plantin [the sixteenth-century spirited and talented printer of the Low Countries]. 'I have a very strong link with Mr. Jones. He was the founder of the Edinburgh Typographia, of which I have the honour to be the Hon. President, succeeding the late Dr. W. Blaikie. I have to ask Mr. Jones to accept this scroll, engrossed on vellum, adorned with the arms of the City of Edinburgh, and the tartan ribbon of the city.

The scroll read as follows:

Many of the friends of Mr. George W. Jones who were associated with him in Edinburgh in his early work for the improvement of typography and the general condition of the printing industry, desire to take this opportunity of expressing their appreciation of his work at that time and their sense of gratification that on this occasion his achievements are being recognised by his fellow printers in London. They are fully conscious of the widespread effect of his early pioneer work and they are satisfied that his influence on his students was not confined to the craft, but extended to their life and character. On behalf of the Edinburgh printers, William Maxwell.

Jones made a reply in the form of a toast to 'The Craft of Printing' and invoked the wonderful history of the trade using names that were never far from his lips: Gutenberg, Schoeffer, Jenson, Manutius, and countless others. His exalted view of the craft of printing was again enunciated.

Some days ago, Miss Clemence Dane, speaking at the Elizabethan Literary Society's Dinner, asked her audience this question: 'What do the Elizabethans think of us?' She said they must be somewhere, because they are immortals. Of course they are somewhere, because they are immortals! But, are they not, most of them, perhaps all of them, immortals because they became so by the agency of the printed word?

His loyalty to friends was expressed at the dinner as well.

May I mention one or two without appearing invidious. My old friend John Northend, of Sheffield, is here bearing the burden of several more than seventy years, and we were friends before we met at Leicester in 1887, to found the British Typographia; Walter Beeby, who is Secretary of the

Northampton Association, who has specially come from that city, worked with me at Leicester in 1887, and helped to print *The British Printer* in the early part of 1888, and to establish my business in 1889. The President of the Federation [William Maxwell], and Mr. William Will, who also is here, were both associated with me in the glorious technical work begun at Edinburgh in 1888. Good friends are of the best of the good gifts of God's bestowing![2]

VISIT TO THE UNITED STATES OF AMERICA

Jones's work as a printer and as a type designer was widely appreciated in the United States of America. He was praised by many of his New World contemporaries, such as William Edwin Rudge, Bruce Rogers, W.A. Dwiggins, William Dana Orcutt, and Carl Purington Rollins. It has been shown that Jones attended a meeting of the International Typographic Council in New York during 1927 and did some lecturing when in the country, promising to do more in the future. His next visit appears to have been in 1930 when he undertook a lecture tour in the company of his daughter, Alice, and William Edwin Rudge.

He arrived in New York on Tuesday 22 September 1930 and departed from the city on Saturday 22 November 1930. Over that two-month period Jones visited Boston, Cleveland, Detroit, Chicago, Minneapolis, Seattle, San Francisco, Los Angeles, New Orleans, Atlanta and Washington. He also went to Vancouver and Winnipeg in Canada, the latter the home of another daughter. It was a strenuous itinerary for any man, but especially so for one in his seventieth year. *The Caxton Magazine* estimated the trip to be 18,700 miles. His exploits were reported in the American and British trade magazines, as well as in some regional American newspapers.

It is clear from the interview given by Jones to *The Caxton Magazine* of February 1931 that he had enjoyed the tour immensely. He met W.A. (Bill) Dwiggins (a designer of many things including typefaces) and Daniel Berkeley Updike (of the Merrymount Press) in Boston; George Carter (the US Government Printer) in Washington; John Henry Nash in San Francisco; and Bill Pfaff (President of the United Typothetae) in New Orleans. He lectured in virtually all the places visited and before some distinguished audiences of the Craftsman's Guild in Winnipeg, the Rowfant Book Club in Cleveland, the Zamorano Book Club in Los Angeles, and Stanford University in San Francisco. At a dinner sponsored by the Printers' Board of Trade in San Francisco, some 350 guests turned up to hear Jones speak, among them the British Consul-General. His words to *The Caxton Magazine* sum up the excitement. 'Everywhere we went we found lunches, dinners, or meetings had been arranged.' When asked why he subjected himself to such a taxing schedule, Jones replied:

I owe a great debt to American printers. When I was a young man in the early 'eighties [1880s], few English printers knew much about printing in its higher flights. Few of us in this country were doing other than very ordinary work. Then came the American invasion of material and appliances. The result was that I got in touch with a number of leading American printers who sent me examples of their work, and in their correspondence gave me much encouragement. We exchanged specimens, and this had a big influence on my work, because this was for a time the only work I could get hold of which possessed characteristics of its own, and so different from ours.[3]

Jones recorded in his *Who's Who* entry, membership of the Zamorano Book Club of Los Angeles, the Roxburghe Book Club of San Francisco, and the Winnipeg branch of the Craftsman's Union.

ROYAL PRINTER AND THE WORCESTERSHIRE REGIMENT

At the outbreak of the First World War, Jones was fifty-four and consequently exempt from any national service. He was a patriot and intensely proud of his country and must have taken a keen interest in current affairs and in the progress of the horrific war.

At some indeterminate time, a distinction was added to his letterheadings: 'By Appointment Printer to Their Majesties The King & Queen of the Belgians', though I have uncovered virtually nothing as to how this honour came about or why it was bestowed. Enquiries to the Belgian authorities have been fruitless. My belief is that the honour arose from the First World War, either because of commercial services provided or because of work in aid of the war wounded.

The only clue I have found is in a piece of job printing promoting the Venezia and Humanistic typefaces as exclusive to the Sign of the Dolphin enterprise, which must have emerged from the presses soon after the war, perhaps in 1919. It is a single-fold, four-page production in two colours. On the fourth and last page is a resetting in Venezia of a letter from J. Ingenbleek, Le Secretaire to Her Majesty the Queen of the Belgians, dated 26 September 1918 and sent from the Belgian Grand Headquarters. The text reads as follows.

Sir, Your homage has greatly pleased the Queen. Her Majesty admires the magnificent printing, which does honour to your presses. She congratulates you on the artistic character of your work, and she thanks you for an attention of which she is particularly sensible.

I am charged to give you the assurance that the portrait and the photogravure which you have presented to our Gracious Sovereign will be well cared for, and I ask you to accept, Sir, the assurance of my distinguished consideration.

Another connection possibly explaining the Belgian recognition was given in the tribute to Jones by Lt Col. R.F. Truscott, OBE, at the seventieth-birthday dinner. His words were recorded in the *Monthly Record* of the London Master Printers' Association in 1930.

George Jones wished that the gallantry of the 2nd Battalion of his county regiment – the Worcesters – at Gheluvelt on October 31, 1914, should be commemorated in a fitting manner. He was instrumental in raising the funds for a memorial and associated it for ever with the 'Homes of Disabled Belgian Soldiers', as it is erected against one of the houses built by that association at Gheluvelt for one of the incapacitated soldiers of our ally.

In 1925 Jones printed an octavo booklet of some thirty pages entitled *Gheluvelt, 31st October 1914. A short account of the Battle of Gheluvelt with Map showing the positions of the Worcestershire Regiment and the Enemy forces on the 31st October 1914.* The text, written by Major B.C. Stenhouse Clarke of the Worcestershire Regiment (Adjutant at the Battle), was set in the then newly-released Linotype Granjon. Both printing and publishing was effected by Jones and the booklet was sold at the memorial in Gheluvelt inaugurated on the eleventh anniversary of the battle in 1925. Copies could also be obtained from the Brussels office of Asiles des Soldat Invalides Belges. The booklet was available not only in English, but also in the two Belgian national languages, Flemish and French. Jones lists the production in his second catalogue of books.

The *Upton News* of 28 November 1925 reported on the unveiling of the memorial.

The memorial erected at Gheluvelt, near Ypres, to men of the second Battalion of the Worcestershire Regiment which contributed to the check of the German advance on 31 October 1914, has been unveiled in the presence of many British and Belgian citizens. The memorial was given by Mr. George W. Jones, formerly of Upton on Severn, and is placed on a house belonging to the National Association of Belgian Mutilated Soldiers.

Jones was unable to attend the inauguration of the memorial because of illness, a fact recorded in the Gheluvelt booklet.

At the unveiling ceremony, Leon Herbos, Director-General of the Homes for Disabled Belgian Soldiers, made a short speech and acknowledged the part played by Jones in erecting the memorial.

A citizen of Great Britain, Mr. George W. Jones, a native of that same county of Worcester from which the heroes of the Battle of Gheluvelt originated, desired that a monument should remind future generations of the brilliant action fought on that day on the land of Gheluvelt. He did not wish a crushing monument; he said to himself that it was sufficient that the memory of the heroes of the Worcestershire Regiment should be engraved on stone and he had the delicate and touching thought of associating disabled Belgian ex-servicemen with this testimony.

When he had conceived this idea, he communicated his intention to Monsieur Henri de Schoonen, who at that time presided over the destiny of the Organisation, Homes for Disabled Belgian Soldiers, and who with all his heart associated himself with the realisation of the scheme. . . .

The Organisation of the Homes for Disabled Belgian Soldiers have been happy and proud to associate themselves intimately with the commemoration desired by Mr. Jones.

To commemorate the gallantry of the Worcestershire Regiment in England, a park in the county town has been named after the battle with suitably inscribed plaques.

CHAPTER 14

Retired Printer

Jones retired in 1938, selling his business to Hunt, Barnard & Co. Ltd, a reputable printing house in Aylesbury. His sons Charles and Fred joined the Board of Directors of the merged enterprise. The last book to be completed under Jones's supervision was the weighty *The Great Chronicle of London*, edited by A.H. Thomas and I.D. Thornley. It bore the imprint of 'The Sign of the Dolphin, London and Aylesbury' and printing probably started in one place and finished in the other.

His retirement began at The Orchard, Castlemorton, Malvern Wells in Worcestershire, followed by a move to the Park View Hotel in Rickmansworth, Hertfordshire, and finally to St Andrew's House Hotel, Droitwich Spa, Worcestershire, where he died on 14 May 1942. He was later interred at the family grave in Northwood where his wife, Eliza Sophia, had been buried in 1912. The grave at the Holy Trinity Church, Rickmansworth Road, Northwood, Middlesex, is marked with a modest stone Celtic cross, with Jones described simply as a Printer which summoned the greatest glory for him.

Jones's considerable and distinguished output as a printer will serve as an adequate monument to his life, but in America a more formal tribute was mounted in the Typographic Library and Museum of the American Type Founders Co. in the form of a stained-glass window (see colour illustration 12). It incorporates one of the many printer's marks used by Jones and carries the legend 'George W. Jones . . . Leader of Printing Art in Britain'. Designed by J. Francois Kaufman of New York for $175, the window now lies in the vaults of the Library at Columbia University.[1] It is time for the window to be retrieved and displayed in memory of a remarkable and almost forgotten printer.

Jones should have died a contented and proud man. He had been fêted royally more than once by his peers. Yet one muses on the significance of a letter sent to Jones on 6 February 1937 by Paul Standard of the Canadian Pacific Railway Company. The imagination of the writer roamed freely. 'If I were a wealthy man instead of a merely impoverished enthusiast for printing, I would commission a series of paintings in which George W. Jones would be the central figure. One would show Jones consulting with his favourite maker of handmade paper; another would show him with his favourite binder; still another would show him receiving his knighthood. This latter may sound prophetic, but nothing seems to me so much of a certainty, unless England has lost all appreciation of true craftsmanship and of simple citizenship.'

Notes

CHAPTER I

1 Henry Lewis Bullen, 'George W. Jones, Master Printer of London', *Inland Printer*, January 1929.

2 Joseph Blumenthal, *Bruce Rogers: A Life in Letters*, W. Thomas Taylor, 1989.

3 Anon, 'Gleanings from Chats with Practical Printers', *The Caxton Magazine*, January 1920.

4 Birth certificate from the District of Malvern in Worcestershire.

5 Notes provided by a local historian of Upton-upon-Severn: Roger W.J. Slater.

6 Register of baptisms for the parish of Upton-upon-Severn.

7 Notes provided by a local historian of Upton-upon-Severn: Roger W.J. Slater.

8 Anon, 'Who's Who in the Printing Trade', *The Master Printers Annual*, British Federation of Master Printers, 1924.

9 A.E. Owen-Jones, 'Fifty Years a Printer', *The Caxton Magazine*, May 1924.

10 Leonard Jay, *A Tribute to the Work of George W. Jones, Master Printer, on the Occasion of His Eightieth Birthday*, Birmingham School of Printing, May 1940.

11 Anon, 'Our Portrait Gallery: No. 6 Geo. W. Jones', *The British Printer*, November/December 1888.

12 Indenture of George W. Jones in the possession of Julia Baylis.

CHAPTER 2

1 Anon, 'F. Russell Baylis Elected Federation President', *Midland Alliance* magazine of the British Federation of Master Printers, May 1952.

2 George W. Jones, *Catalogue of the Library of George W. Jones at the Sign of the Dolphin*, George W. Jones, 1938.

3 Roy Millington, *A History of J.W. Northend Ltd, Printers of Sheffield 1889–1989*, J.W. Northend Ltd, 1989.

4 G. Wakeman and G.D.R. Bridson, *A Guide to Nineteenth Century Colour Printers*, The Plough Press, 1975.

5 Roy Millington, *A History of J.W. Northend Ltd, Printers of Sheffield 1889–1989*, J.W. Northend Ltd, 1989.

6 George W. Jones, *Catalogue of the Library of George W. Jones at the Sign of the Dolphin*, 1938.

7 Anon, 'Sheffield Printers' Celebrations', *The Caxton Magazine*, April 1925.

8 Anon [Roy Brewer], *Raithby Lawrence 1876–1976*, Raithby, Lawrence & Co. Ltd, 1976.

9 G. Wakeman and G.D.R. Bridson, *A Guide to Nineteenth Century Colour Printers*, The Plough Press, 1975.

10 Anon, 'Our Portrait Gallery: No. 6 Geo. W. Jones', *The British Printer*, November/December 1888.

11 Vivian Ridler, 'Artistic Printing: a search for principles', *Alphabet and Image*, January 1948.

12 Sean Jennett, 'Printers' International Specimen Exchange 1880–1898', *The British Printer*, December 1957.

13 Anon, 'Our Portrait Gallery: No. 6 Geo. W. Jones', *The British Printer*, November/December 1888.

14 Vivian Ridler, 'Artistic Printing: a search for principles', *Alphabet and Image*, January 1948.

15 Anon, 'Specimens', *The British Printer*, March/April 1889.

16 Anon, 'Specimens', *The British Printer*, January/February 1889.

17 Anon, *Linotype Record*, August 1922.

18 Anon, 'Our Portrait Gallery: No. 11 Thomas I. Burton', *The British Printer*, July/August 1889.

19 Anon, *The British Typographia*. A brochure, 1887.

20 W. Turner Berry and H. Edmund Poole, *Annals of Printing: a Chronological Encyclopaedia*, Blandford Press, 1966.

21 Anon, 'The Guild Movement in England', *The Caxton Magazine*, October 1922.

22 Anon, *The British Typographia*. A brochure, 1887.

23 Anon, 'The First Annual Meeting', *The British Printer*, September/October 1888.

24 Anon, 'Annual Report 1888–89', *The British Printer*, September/October 1888.

25 Anon, 'Raithby, Lawrence & Co. Ltd, v. Hilton', *The British Printer*, November/December 1894.

26 Anon [Roy Brewer], *Raithby Lawrence*

1876–1976, Raithby, Lawrence & Co. Ltd, 1976.

27 Letter from George W. Jones to J.W. Northend of Sheffield (quoted with the permission of T.G. Dakin, Chairman/Managing Director of J.W. Northend Ltd of Sheffield), dated 19 June 1888.

28 Anon, 'Personal', *The British Printer*, March/April 1888.

29 Letter from Green & McAllan, Card Merchants to George W. Jones, dated 20 October 1887.

30 Letter from Harry Copeland to Harry Whetton (Editor of *The British Printer*), dated 14 September 1938.

31 George W. Jones, *Catalogue of the Library of George W. Jones at the Sign of the Dolphin*, George W. Jones, 1938.

32 Anon, 'Personal', *The British Printer*, March/April 1888.

33 Letter from George W. Jones to J.W. Northend of Sheffield, dated 19 June 1888.

34 Anon [Roy Brewer], *Raithby Lawrence 1876–1976*, Raithby, Lawrence & Co. Ltd, 1976.

35 Letter from George W. Jones to J.W. Northend of Sheffield, dated 19 June 1888.

36 Briefing notes written by George W. Jones for Leonard Jay, c.1940.

37 The Darien Press, *Artistic Letterpress Printing*, 1889.

38 Anon, 'Specimens', *The British Printer*, July/August 1888.

39 Anon, 'Specimens', *The British Printer*, November/December 1888.

40 Harold Hood, FRPS, 'The Dissecting Table', *The British Printer*, September/October 1920.

41 Anon, 'Technical Classes', *The British Printer*, November/December 1888.

42 Briefing notes written by George W. Jones for Leonard Jay, c.1940.

43 Anon, 'Technical Classes', *The British Printer*, November/December 1888.

44 Anon, 'An Exhibition of Fine Printing', *The British Printer*, November/December 1888.

45 Anon, 'Minto House Class of Typography, Edinburgh', *The British Printer*, May/June 1889.

46 James Shand, 'Author and Printer: G.B.S. and R. & R.C.: 1898–1948', *Alphabet and Image 8*, December 1948.

47 Anon, 'Distribution of Prizes', *The British Printer*, November/December 1889.

48 Anon, 'Class in Typography – Selkirk', *The British Printer*, November/December 1889.

49 George W. Jones, 'Messrs. George Lewis & Son', *The Printing World*, November 1891.

CHAPTER 3

1 Advertisement for the Grapho Press in *The British Printer*, May/June 1889.

2 Anon, 'Trade Notes', *The British Printer*, July/August 1889.

3 Letter from George W. Jones to J.W. Northend of Sheffield, dated 26 July 1889.

4 Letter from George W. Jones to J.W. Northend of Sheffield, dated August 1889.

5 George W. Jones, *Catalogue of the Library of George W. Jones at the Sign of the Dolphin*, George W. Jones, 1938.

6 Advertisement for Geo. W. Jones in *The British Printer*, September/October 1889.

7 George W. Jones, 'The Late Edward L. Shanks, Typefounder', *The Caxton Magazine*, February 1927.

8 Anon, 'Trade Notes', *The British Printer*, September/October 1889.

9 Anon, 'The "Printing World" Outing', *The Printing World*, July 1907.

10 Advertisement for Geo. W. Jones in *The British Printer*, November/December 1889.

11 Anon, 'Trade Notes', *The British Printer*, November/December 1889.

12 Anon, 'The International Fine Printing Exhibition', *The British Printer*, September/October 1889.

13 Briefing notes written by George W. Jones for Leonard Jay, c.1940.

14 Anon, 'Technical Classes in London', *The British Printer*, November/December 1889.

15 Anon, 'Metropolitan Typographic Classes', *The British Printer*, January/February 1890.

16 Anon, 'The City Technical Classes', *The British Printer*, May/June 1890.

17 Anon, 'Mr. W.H. Slater', *The Printing World*, September 1894.

18 Announcement in *The Printing World*, April 1891.

19 Editorial in *The Printing World*, January 1892.

20 Editorial in *The Printing World*, March 1892.

21 Anon, 'Calendars', *The Caxton Magazine*, April 1922.

22 Readers, 'Praise for Our Printer', *The Printing World*, March 1892.

23 Advertisement for Geo. W. Jones in *The Printing World*, October 1894.

24 Advertisement for Geo. W. Jones in *The Printing World*, May 1893.

25 Advertisement for Geo. W. Jones in *The Printing World*, 1898.

26 Ian Rogerson, *George W. Jones: Master of Master Printers 1860–1942*. An exhibition catalogue. Manchester Metropolitan University Library, 1993.

27 Anon, 'Mr. Geo. W. Jones and the Norwich Typographia', *The Printing World*, May 1897.

(Attributed to the *British and Colonial Printer and Stationer*.)

28 Anon, 'Mr. H.L. Bullen on Type – Mr. Geo. W. Jones on William Morris', *The Caxton Magazine*, April 1924.

29 Editorial, *The Caxton Magazine*, July 1924.

30 George W. Jones, 'Craftsmanship and the Printer', *The Caxton Magazine*, May 1925.

31 George W. Jones, 'An Interview with William Morris', *The Caxton Magazine*, April 1931.

32 Small advertisement in *The Printing World*, February 1897.

33 Anon, ' "The Printing World" Staff Dinner', *The Printing World*, April 1898.

34 Anon, ' "The Printing World" Wayzgoose', *The Printing World*, August 1901.

35 Anon, 'Trade News and Notes', *The Printing World*, October 1907.

36 Anon, 'Trade Unionism and Litigation', *The Printing World*, May 1899.

CHAPTER 4

1 John Southward, 'Progress in Printing and the Graphic Arts during the Victorian Era,' *The Printing World*, December 1897.

2 L.W. Wallis, *A Concise Chronology of Typesetting Developments 1886–1986*, Lund Humphries, 1988.

3 Theodore L. De Vinne, 'A Good Testimonial', *The Printing World*, November 1902.

4 Letter from James Shand to George W. Jones of 3 May 1937.

5 Anon, 'Linotype Typography', *The Linotype Record*, January 1922.

6 Advertisement of the Linotype Co. Ltd in *The Printing World*, August 1910.

7 James Moran, *Printing Presses,* Faber & Faber, 1973.

8 Anon, 'A Striking Advertisement', *The Printing World*, September 1900.

9 W. Turner Berry and H. Edmund Poole, *Annals of Printing: a Chronological Encyclopaedia*, Blandford Press, 1966.

10 Advertisement for Josiah Wade Ltd in *The Printing World*, July 1894.

11 Advertisement for W.E. Cook in *The Printing World*, September 1894.

12 Advertisement for Parsons, Fletcher & Co. in *The Printing World*, September 1894.

13 Advertisement for Dalziel Foundry Ltd in *The British Printer*, June/July 1919.

CHAPTER 5

1 Anon, 'Colour Printing Today', *The British Printer*, April/May 1907.

2 H.M. Cartwright, *Photo-engraving,* Ilford Ltd, 1961.

3 W. Turner Berry and H. Edmund Poole,

Annals of Printing: a Chronological Encyclopaedia, Blandford Press, 1966.

4 Anon, *Adam & Charles Black 1807–1957*, Adam & Charles Black, 1957.

5 Colin Inman, *The A & C Black Colour Books*, Werner Shaw Ltd, 1990.

6 Anon, *Adam & Charles Black 1807–1957*, Adam & Charles Black, 1957.

7 George W. Jones, *Catalogue of the Library of George W. Jones at the Sign of the Dolphin*, George W. Jones, 1938.

8 Advertisement for George W. Jones Ltd in *The Printing World*, January 1907.

9 Anon, 'Three-colour Printing', *The Printing World*, April 1903.

10 Ibid.

11 Anon, 'Brevities', *The Process Engravers Monthly*, May 1907.

12 Advertisement for Geo. W. Jones Ltd in *The Printing World*, May 1906.

13 Anonymous small advertisement in *The Printing World*, April 1907.

14 Anon, 'In the Printing World', *The Printing Machinery Record*, February 1908.

15 Anon, *The Menpes Printing Company Ltd*. A booklet in the St Bride Printing Library, 1909.

16 Anon, 'Junior Institution of Engineers', *The Printing World*, April 1909.

17 Anon, 'The Romance of Colour Printing', *The Printing World*, February 1902.

18 Anon, 'News', *The Printing World*, January 1907.

19 Colour supplement, 'A Bit of Old Worcester' in *The Printing World*, January 1906.

20 George W. Jones, *Catalogue of the Library of George W. Jones at the Sign of the Dolphin,* George W. Jones, 1938.

21 Ian Rogerson, *George W. Jones, Master of Master Printers 1860–1942.* An exhibition catalogue. Manchester Metropolitan University Library, 1993.

22 Leonard Jay, *A Tribute to the Work of George W. Jones, Master Printer, on the Occasion of His Eightieth Birthday*, Birmingham School of Printing, 1940.

CHAPTER 6

1 Anon, 'Presentation at Cassiobury Press', *Linotype Notes*, September 1907.

2 Anon, ' "The Printing World" Outing', *The Printing World*, July 1907.

3 Anon, 'The Menpes Press Sports', *The Printing World*, July 1908.

4 George Mortimer, 'A Personality in British Printing', *The Printing Art*, September 1912.

5 S. Humphries, *Oriental Carpets, Runners and Rugs*, Adam & Charles Black, 1910.

6 Obituary, Mr Mortimer Menpes, *The Times*, 5 April 1938.

7   Anon, *The Master Printer,* 1908.

8   Anon, 'Random Pars', *Linotype Notes,* May 1910.

9   Anon, 'City of London Printers' Musical Society', *Linotype Notes,* November 1910.

10 Anon, 'George W. Jones, Common Councillor', *The British Printer,* May/June 1923.

CHAPTER 7

1   Colour insert to *Linotype Notes,* July 1911.

2   Anon, 'The "Caxton" Reviews', *The Caxton Magazine,* January 1912.

3   F.C. Avis, *Edward Philip Prince, Type Punch-cutter,* F.C. Avis, 1967.

4   *The Shakespeare Tercentenary Meeting held at the Mansion House on May Day 1916.* Booklet printed by G.W. Jones in 1916.

5   George W. Jones, 'The Late Edward L. Shanks, Typefounder', *The Caxton Magazine,* February 1927.

6   P.M. Shanks & Sons Ltd, *Specimens of Printing Types.* Not dated.

7   Anon, 'Specimens for Review', *The British Printer,* August/September 1916.

8   B.H. Newdigate, 'Some Type Faces for Books', *The London Mercury,* March 1921.

9   Various hands, 'Postscripts on Dwiggins', *Typophile Chap Book No. 36,* 1960.

CHAPTER 8

1   Anon, 'A Parliamentary Committee on Display Type!', *The British Printer,* May/June 1920.

2   Anon, 'Reform of Government Printing', *The Caxton Magazine,* September 1922.

3   B.H. Newdigate, 'Book Production Notes', *The London Mercury,* August 1920.

4   Anon, *Report of the Committee appointed to Select the Best Faces of Type and Modes of Display for Government Printing,* HMSO, 1922.

5   Anon, 'Reform of Government Printing', *The Caxton Magazine,* September 1922.

6   Walter Tracy, *Letters of Credit,* Gordon Fraser, 1986.

7   Anon, 'An Art Director for the Monotype', *The Caxton Magazine,* March 1921.

8   F. Colebrook, 'The Commercial Value of Beauty', *The Caxton Magazine,* June 1920.

9   Letter from Walter Tracy to James Moran, dated 9 October 1970, in the St Bride Printing Library.

10 Letter from Walter Tracy to James Moran, dated 23 September 1970, in the St Bride Printing Library.

11 Leonard Jay, *Si Monumentum Requiris, Circumspice: notes on the Libraries of George W. Jones, Esq.,* Birmingham School of Printing, 1942.

12 Anon, 'Reviews', *The Caxton Magazine,* May 1922.

13 Anon, 'Editorial', *The Caxton Magazine,* May 1922.

CHAPTER 9

1   Anon, 'Mr. George W. Jones and the Linotype Record', *The Caxton Magazine,* December 1924.

2   Anon, 'Granjon Old Face & Decoration of this Issue', *The Linotype Record,* April 1925.

3   Conversation between Alan Shelley (formerly of Linotype) and L.W. Wallis in the autumn of 1992.

4   Paul Beaujon, 'The Garamond Types', *The Fleuron,* No. V, 1926.

5   B.H. Newdigate, 'Mr. B.H. Newdigate on Linotype "Granjon" and "Venezia" Types', *The Linotype Record,* 1926.

6   *The Printer and Bookmaker* quoted in *Linotype Notes,* 20 September 1898.

7   Letter from C.H. Griffith to G.W. Jones, dated 28 March 1929, in the archive of the Mergenthaler Linotype Co.

8   Hugh Williamson, *Methods of Book Design,* Oxford University Press, 1956.

9   Conversation between Alan Shelley (formerly of Linotype) and L.W. Wallis in 1993.

10 Rita D. Jacobs, 'Signage with Sense, not Signature', *Graphis,* July/August 1991.

11 Irvin Haas, *Bruce Rogers: A Bibliography,* Kennikat Press 1968.

12 Carl Purington Rollins, 'The Psalms of David', *Publishers' Weekly,* 2 June 1928.

13 A.F. Johnson, *Type Designs, their history and development,* Andre Deutsch, 1966.

14 W. Pincus Jaspert, W. Turner Berry and A.F. Johnson, *The Encyclopedia of Type Faces,* Blandford Press, 1970.

15 Walter Tracy, *Letters of Credit,* Gordon Fraser, 1986.

16 Letter from Walter Tracy to James Moran, dated 17 April 1970, in the St Bride Printing Library.

17 Hugh Williamson, *Methods of Book Design,* Oxford University, 1956.

18 William J. Glick, *William Edwin Rudge,* The Typophiles, 1984.

19 Joseph Blumenthal, *Bruce Rogers: A Life in Letters,* W. Thomas Taylor, 1989.

20 John Dreyfus, *The Survival of Baskerville's Punches,* Cambridge University Press, 1949.

21 Walter Tracy, *Letters of Credit,* Gordon Fraser, 1986.

22 Anon, 'Baskerville', *Linotype Matrix,* Summer 1950.

23 George W. Jones, *Catalogue of the Library of George W. Jones at the Sign of the Dolphin,* George W. Jones, 1938.

24 B.H. Newdigate, *The London Mercury,* November 1931.

25 Leonard Jay, 'On the Acquirement of a Collection of Wood Engravings from the Press at the Sign of the Dolphin', *Torch No. 2*, Birmingham School of Printing, 1938.

26 A.F. Johnson, 'Some English Decorated Initials', *Alphabet and Image* 7, May 1948.

27 Anon, 'An International Typographic Council Formed for World-Wide Service', *The Printing Craftsman*, April 1926.

28 Anon, 'Form International Typographic Council to Solve World-Wide Linotype Problems', *Ben Franklin and Western Printing*, 15 March 1926.

29 Notebooks of Fritz Max Steltzer, in possession of Monotype Typography Ltd.

30 George W. Jones, 'Building Men for the Noblest of Crafts', *The Caxton Magazine*, October 1927

CHAPTER 10

1 Leonard Jay, *Si Monumentum Requiris, Circumspice: notes on the Libraries of George W. Jones, Esq.*, Birmingham School of Printing, 1942.

2 Sotheby & Co., *Catalogue of the Well-Known Collection of Rare and Valuable Books Illustrating the History of Printing formed by George W. Jones, Esq., Monkbarns, Northwood, Middlesex*, annotated in pencil by Leonard Jay, 1936.

3 R.B. Fishenden, 'Library of a Master Printer', *The Caxton Magazine*, August 1936.

4 George W. Jones, *Catalogue of the Library of George W. Jones at the Sign of the Dolphin*, George W. Jones, 1938.

5 Letter from H.G. Clarke to Leonard Jay, dated 30 October 1942, in the possession of L.W. Wallis.

CHAPTER 11

1 Joseph Thorp, 'Betraying "The Mystery"', *Printing Review*, 1945.

2 B.H. Newdigate, 'Two Centuries of Type-Founding', *The London Mercury*, July 1921.

3 Anon, ' "The Caxton" Reviews', *The Caxton Magazine*, May 1921.

4 Ian Rogerson, *George W. Jones, Master of Master Printers 1860–1942*. An exhibition catalogue. Manchester Metropolitan University Library, 1993.

5 John Dreyfus, 'Dennis Cohen and The Cresset Press', *Matrix 13*, Winter 1992.

6 *The Times Literary Supplement*, 5 February 1931.

7 B.H. Newdigate, 'Machine Composition at Its Best', *The London Mercury*, January 1923.

8 Anon, 'The Deserted Village', *The Caxton Magazine*, April 1922.

9 *The Times Literary Supplement*, 11 September 1930.

10 George W. Jones, *Catalogue of the Library of George W. Jones at the Sign of the Dolphin*, 1938.

11 John Dreyfus, *A History of the Nonesuch Press*, The Nonesuch Press, 1981.

12 Anon, 'A Fine Piece of Book Printing', *The Caxton Magazine*, April 1925.

13 *The Times Literary Supplement*, 11 September 1930.

14 B.H. Newdigate, 'Book Production Notes', *The London Mercury*, April 1932.

CHAPTER 12

1 Oliver Simon, *Printer and Playground*, Faber & Faber, 1956.

2 Herbert Simon, *Song and Words: a history of the Curwen Press*, George Allen & Unwin, 1973.

3 James Moran, *Stanley Morison: His typographic achievement*, Lund Humphries, 1971.

4 Nicolas Barker, *Stanley Morison*, Macmillan, 1972.

5 James Moran, *The Double Crown Club*, Westerham Press, 1974.

6 Anon, 'The "Times" Printing Number', *The Caxton Magazine*, November 1929.

7 Herbert Simon, *Song and Words: a history of the Curwen Press*, George Allen & Unwin, 1973.

8 Sotheby & Co., *Catalogue of the Well-Known Collection of Rare and Valuable Books Illustrating the History of Printing formed by George W. Jones, Esq.*, 1936.

9 Nicolas Barker, *Stanley Morison*, Macmillan, 1972.

10 Letter from Stanley Morison to G.W. Jones, dated 12 July 1938.

11 Anon, 'London Printing Craftsmen', *The Caxton Magazine*, May 1930.

CHAPTER 13

1 Anon, 'Craft Jubilee Dinner', *The Caxton Magazine*, July 1924.

2 Anon, 'Our Printer Laureate', *The Caxton Magazine*, June 1930.

3 A.E. Owen-Jones, 'George W. Jones does a propaganda trip of 18,700 miles', *The Caxton Magazine*, February 1931.

CHAPTER 14

1 Letter from Francine Corcione of the Jersey City Museum to L.W. Wallis, dated 11 January 1993.

Index

Figures in *italics* refer to monochrome
illustrations unless otherwise stated

A. & C. Black 8, 49–51, 89, 99
American Type Founders Company 9, 69, 76, 92,
    111, 120; *col. illus. 12*
Aquila Press 99, *102*, 103
Art Nouveau 34
artistic printing 13–16, 20, 34–5
Arts and Crafts Movement 34

Bartlett, E. 66, 91, 114
Baskerville (typeface) 7, *80*, 81–7, 92, 97
Bassett, J. 31–2, 34
Beeby, W. 21, 110, 115
Bernard (typeface) 72, 74
Birmingham School of Printing 8, 11, 55, 68, 89,
    96–7
Bodoni (typeface) 42, 103
British Printer, The 17, 19, *19*, 20–3, 25, 27, 29, 36,
    45–6, 48, 60, 111, 114, 116
British Typographia 16–17, *18*, *19*, 20, 24, 30, 115
Bullen, H.L. 9, 34, 111

Caslon (typeface) 14, 36, 65, 72, 83–4, 101
Caxton Magazine, The 17, 34, 36, 65, 66, 67, 70,
    96, 101, 103, 106, 114, 116–17
Civilité (typeface) 75–6, *95*, 96, 103, 106
Co-operative Printing Company 22
cylinder press 22, 44

Darien Press 23–4, 30
decoration 14, 34, 67, 89–90, *90*
Dreyfus, J. 8, 9, 102
Dwiggins, W.A. 63, 85–6, 89, 114, 116

Ebenezer Baylis & Son Ltd 7, 11–12, 97
Estienne (typeface) 76–8, *78*, 79, 81, 85, 96–7, *102*,
    103–4, 106, 114; *col. illus. 9*

Garamond (typeface) 69, 75, 78, 83, 92
Geo. W. Jones Ltd (later Cassiobury Press and
    Menpes Press) 28–9, 31, 33, 37, 39, 49–50,
    52–3, *53*, 56–7; *col. illus. 1*
Georgian (typeface) 85, 87, *88*, 89, 97
Goudy, F.W. 65, 76
Granjon (typeface) 6, 69, 70, 71–2, 73, 74–6, 85,
    97, *101*, 102, 105, 118–19; *col. illus. 8*,
    col. illus. 11
Grapho Press 27–8, *28*, 29–30, 62
Griffith, C.H. 63, 71, 74, 79, 81–7

Hartley & Son Ltd 12
Hilton, R. 16–17, 19–21, 24–6, 29
Humanistic (typeface) 63, 118; *col. illus. 7*

International Exhibition of Fine Printing 29–30
International Typographic Council 90–2, 116

Jay, L. 8, 11, 55, 68, 89, 93, 97
Jones, G.W.
    apprentice 6, 9–12
    birth 9
    collector 35–6, 67, 93–8, 109–10
    eightieth birthday 55
    employer 37–8
    exhibitions 24–5
    family 10
    freemason *58*, *59*, 104
    ill health 12
    infant home 6, 10, *10*
    marriage 13
    non-commercial appointments 59–60;
        col. illus. 4
    retirement 93, 120
    seventieth birthday 8, 110, 113–16, 118
    silver wedding anniversary 57
    teacher 24–6, 30
    trade training 6, 11
    Treasury committee 64–5
    tributes to 111, 120; *col. illus. 12*
    typographic style 34–5, 67
    Worcestershire regiment 7, 118–19
J.W. Northend Ltd 7

Lanston Monotype Corporation 6, 9, 36, 65,
    67–9, 107, 113
Leicester Free Style 16
Limited Editions Club 55, 74, 81, 97, 99, 105;
    col. illus. 10, *col. illus. 11*
Linotype machine 39–40, *40*, 41–3, 48, 68–9,
    71–2, 104; *col. illus. 9*
Linotype & Machinery Ltd 7, 36, 42, 66, *66*, 68,
    71, 74, 78, *78*, 79, 81–3, 85–7, 99, 100, 103,
    106 111, 113; *col. illus. 8*

Linotype Notes 42, 61; *col. illus. 5*
Linotype Record, The 15, *15*, 42, 67–9, *73*, 76,
    77, 78
Linotype typography 8, 45, 62, 64–6, 69, 72, 75–6,
    83, 86–7, 91–2, 107
London College of Printing 9
London Master Printers' Association 110, 113,
    118
London Society of Compositors 38, 112

Menpes, M. 49, 51–2, 59
Mergenthaler Linotype Company 41, 63, 71, 74,
    79, 81–2, 97, 114
Miehle machine 6, 13, *43*, 43–8. 52
Monotype machine 68
Monotype Recorder, The 67–8
Monotype typography 7, 41, 45, 64–5, 104
Morison, S. 6, 9, 36, 67, 83, 104, 106, 107–10, 113
Morris, W. *33*, 34–5, 39, 61, 94

Newdigate, B. 62–4, 71–2, 86, 89, 100–1, 104
Nonesuch Press 97, 104; *col. illus. 9*
Northend, J.W. 7, 13, 20, 27–8, 100, 111, 113, 115

Orcutt, W.D. 63, 81, 116; *col. illus. 7*

Paper and Printing Trades Journal, The 14, 20
Pawson & Brailsford Ltd 12
platen press 15, 22, 46, 52
    Arab 21, *44*, 45–6
    Armoury 45, 49
    Golding Jobber 21
    Mitre 45
    Reddish Jobber 45
Printers' International Specimen Exchange 13–14,
    15, 16, 20, 25, 93
printing process

colour reproduction 48–56, 59
handpress 11–12
letterpress 6, 9, 11–12, 36, 43–4, 48–9, 66–7,
    101
    polychromatic 48, 101
    trichromatic 43, 48–54, 61; *col illus. 3*
lithography 49, 51
power press 12
Printing World, The 31–2, *32*, 33, *33*, 34, 36–8,
    41–2, 45, 48–9, 53–4, 56–7; *col. illus. 2*

Raithby & Lawrence 13, 16–17, 19–22, 30
Riddell, J.R. 9, 110–11
Rogers, B. 6, 9, 75, 81, 83–4, 94, 97, 109, 116
Rudge, W.E. 75, 79, 81–2, 84–7, 97, 114, 116

Shanks, E. 28–9, 62
Sheffield Daily Telegraph 12
Sign of the Dolphin Press 55, 61–3, 79, 89, *90*,
    94, *95*, 97, 99, 103, 106–7, 110, 118, 120;
    col. illus. 5
St Bride Foundation Institute 59
St Bride Foundation Printing School 9, 59
Sun Engraving Co. Ltd (previously Menpes
    Printing and Engraving Co. Ltd and
    André, Sleigh & Anglo Ltd) 53, 59

Typographical Association 12

Upton-upon-Severn 6, 8–10, *10*, 119

Venezia (typeface) 61–2, *63*, 65, 76, 97, 106, 118;
    col. illus. 6

Warde, B. 9, 71–2, 104, 110, 113
Wharfedales 44
Whetton, H. 22, 38, 111